America's Children:

TRIUMPH or TRAGEDY

America's Children:

TRIUMPH or TRAGEDY

BY

Charles N. Oberg, MD, MPH

Nicholas A. Bryant

Marilyn L. Bach, PhD

American Public Health Association
1015 Fifteenth Street, NW
Washington, DC 20005

Design: Teddie Barnhart, Barnstorming Designs, Frederick, MD
Illustration: Scott Roberts, Bel Air, MD
Typesetting: Litho Comp, Bethesda, MD
Set in: Garamond Light Condensed

ISBN 0-87553-218-7

3/M 11/94

CONTENTS

PREFACE

America's children are in a state of crisis. Their representation among the poor and disadvantaged has grown at an unprecedented rate. Although the legacy of the 1980s and of the Reagan years has yet to be fully realized, it is apparent now that the erroneous economic policies of those years have created severe fiscal problems for our nation. Children's services have been grossly underfunded and underrepresented among a multitude of social service agencies at the federal, state, and local levels.

An underfunded and fragmented approach to children's services is no longer acceptable and does not address the growing concerns of many public health professionals. Unless we recognize the multiple and interrelated needs of our children, it will be difficult to reverse present trends. Realizing that caring for our richest natural resource—our children—is an investment in the truest sense of the word, we need to develop a new "social will" and make a renewed commitment to change.

The former Soviet Union's 1957 launching of Sputnik threatened the security of the United States. Because the potential ramifications of Sputnik's technology ignited a frenzy of fear, the United States made a focused commitment to national defense: The National Defense Education Act of 1958 provided substantial federal funds for the qualitative and quantitative improvement in technology and galvanized our country's dedication to science, which resulted in our placing a man on the moon 11 years later.

Once again our country is being threatened. This time the threat is not from the outside—as was the case with Sputnik—but from within. The current deterioration of our youth threatens to destroy our country. Although this threat does not carry the ominous possibilities of nuclear war as did the Soviet challenge in 1957, it does place our nation's rich legacy at risk.

The tragic cases presented in the following chapters are an indictment of our public policy and politics during the past 15 years. The blame must be shared by presidents, Congress, policy-makers, and every American. The time has come to redirect our focus and reinvigorate our efforts to nurture each individual child so that he or she may triumph over adversity rather than fail because of public neglect. We must save our children before it is too late.

It is tragic that this book had to be written.

—CHARLES N. OBERG, MD, MPH
NICHOLAS A. BRYANT
MARILYN L. BACH, PhD

ACKNOWLEDGMENTS

Many individuals and organizations made this book possible. However, we must thank several authors on whose work this book builds. We recognize the contribution of the late Michael Harrington, who first opened our eyes to *The Other America: Poverty in the United States*. He demonstrated that an individual's concern and vision can make a difference. We also thank Jonathon Kozol, who crystallized the human impact of homelessness in *Rachel and Her Children: Homeless Families in America*, and Lisbeth Schorr, who dared us to break the cycle of poverty and despair in *Within Our Reach: Breaking the Cycle of Disadvantage*.

The commitment and support from the American Public Health Association has been exceptional, particularly from Sabine J. Beisler, publications services director, and Cheryl N. Jackson, production manager, who gave the manuscript life. A very special thanks goes to Anne Zimmer, who, as our liaison to the APHA Publications Board, guided this project from start to finish. We thank David Mottet of Biomedical Graphics, University of Minnesota for his graphic design assistance. We also thank Dr. Arthur Caplan at the University of Pennsylvania, for his support and encouragement. Dr. Oberg would especially like to thank his wife Linda for her love and support.

We thank our own children, Elizabeth, Kathryn, David, Peter, Wendy, Maya Lucey, and Vito, and hope that all children have the opportunity not only to live, but also to enjoy and cherish life's joy. Finally, we send forth a plea for the infant at the Plaza—let us never forget nor walk on by.

INTRODUCTION

> " Between the idea...
>
> And the reality...
>
> Between the
>
> motion...
>
> And the act...
>
> Falls the shadow."
>
> —T. S. ELIOT

Several years ago, while I was attending an American Public Health Association (APHA) conference in New York, the invisible status of our poor children left an indelible impression on me. It was dusk when a friend and I decided to stroll up Broadway to Central Park. Enthralled by the bright neon lights and the fast-moving crowds, we had just passed the famous Plaza Hotel, a symbol of affluence, when I noticed a shadowy figure in the dark. It was a woman, huddled in the cold and damp. This woman was far different from the numerous panhandlers who had previously approached us. She sat silent and expressionless, wrapped in a torn, brown blanket. There was a small cardboard box at her side. Inside the box, which was lined with a tattered cloth, slept an infant. It looked cold, ill, and malnourished. I hate to admit that we walked past them in silence, offering no support or assistance. At the corner we met a police officer and told him of the woman and infant, but he seemed uninterested.

Because of the utter helplessness I felt that night, the image of that woman and infant haunts me to this day. Such a scenario is not uncommon in the cities and small, rural communities of the United States. Many women and their children live in an austere and insular poverty, lacking life's basic necessities of food, shelter, access to medical care, affordable child care, and early education services. They have become alienated and disenfranchised from the rest of the population. What is the life potential for the infant outside the Plaza Hotel? If this child survives, what does his or her future hold?

In the Greek tragedies of Sophocles and Euripides it is not the evildoer who suffers a grievous fate; rather, it is the virtuous and courageous who meet a tragic end because of an isolated, unseen flaw. The neglect of our children is the tragic flaw of our society. If left uncorrected, it could have irreversible repercussions.

The US Constitution speaks of our nation's many virtues—a government based on equal representation, freedom of speech and religion, civil rights, and a judicial system that maintains one's innocence until proven guilty. Yet what of our children—our neglected future—who lack life's basic necessities? The undervaluing of our children is a hidden flaw that will surface in the next generation and possibly lead to our national decline and demise: a demise brought about not by an invasion from abroad but by a deterioration from within.

Many may consider this position to be a distorted, alarmist attitude that exaggerates the extent of the problem. What makes our case so compelling, however, is the juxtaposition of two divergent trends whose interplay will make the crisis more apparent in the near future. The first is the aging of our population. At the turn of the century, persons over the age of 65 represented only 4% of the population; by 1990 this population had increased to 12%.[1] Seniors over the age of 85 are the fastest growing segment of our population. At present, they constitute only 1% of the population, but they will represent close to 2% by the year 2000 and may exceed 5% by 2050.[2] The second major trend is the impoverishment of children. The Census Bureau calculated that the poverty rate among children in 1992 was at 21.9%, which means over 14 million children live in poverty.[3] The rate

for black children living in poverty is over 40%, and the rate for Hispanic children is almost as high.[4]

How do the two trends relate? Simply stated, children become adults, and adults must become productive members of our society to carry on its legacy. What do we know about the demographics of our children? First, fertility rates in this country are insufficient to replace the current population. In other words, when the "baby boomers" reach their golden years, our nation will be experiencing an ongoing reduction in the number of active adults who can run the country and support the elderly population. It is estimated that as the baby boomers age, the elderly population will grow fourfold by 2050. After 2000, there will be more old people than young for the first time in US history.[5] As the number of people drawing Social Security increases, the number of workers contributing to the Society Security fund will continued to dwindle. In 1950, there were 16 workers for every retiree. By 1960, the ratio had decreased to 5 workers per retiree. It is estimated that by the year 2034 there will be only 2 workers per retiree.[6]

Thus, the United States is faced with an aging population in need of a vibrant and efficient work force for the next century and with a childhood population that is becoming more vulnerable and at risk. Because of this, the fact of children in poverty must be addressed. But the social welfare programs designed to alleviate children's poverty were decimated in the 1980s. The massive reduction in social support services is evident in the areas of health care, nutritional support, child care, and early education services.

The Greek tragedies mentioned above were brought about by a character flaw in the protagonist. If our society does not address the many problems facing its children, the United States will also suffer a tragic fate. If recognized early enough, however, the course can be changed.

A renewed agenda for the health and welfare of our children not only is the proper moral decision but is necessary for the health and welfare of the United States. Although the premise of this book is based on the economic reality of poverty and its consequences, we must never forget the inherent value of children and their right to grow and develop to their full potential.

Chuck Oberg, MPH

References

1. *Aging America, Trends and Projections, 1987–1988 Edition.* Washington, DC; US Senate Special Committee on Aging. R 3377, 1988:8.
2. Suzman R, Riley MW. Introducing the "Oldest Old." *Milbank Q.* 1985;63(2):177–186.
3. *Poverty in the United States: 1992.* Washington, DC: US Bureau of the Census, 1993:4. Current Population Reports, P. 60 ser., no. 185.
4. *Statistical Abstract of the United States: 1992.* Washington, DC: US Bureau of the Census; 1992: Table 3.
5. *America in the 21st Century: Human Resources Development.* Washington, DC: Population Reference Bureau; February, 1990.
6. *Beyond Rhetoric: A New American Agenda for Children and Families,* Washington, DC: The National Commission on Children; 1991:17.

Building for
the Future

> *"The child is father of the man..."*
>
> **—WILLIAM WORDSWORTH**

Responsibility for children's services is spread among many advocacy organizations, social service agencies, and numerous departments within our government. This lack of conceptual integration is evident at the federal, state, and local levels of society. Because programs and issues relevant to children have been fragmented and uncoordinated, children's services must often compete for limited funds in this time of fiscal constraint. A fragmented approach is no longer acceptable to many health and developmental experts. Unless there is a realization of the multiple and interrelated needs of our children, the reversal of present trends will be difficult to achieve. We need to develop a unifying paradigm to scrutinize the allocation of resources and to optimize their distribution and use.

There is a common tendency to equate children's health with access to high-quality medical care. Medical care is but one variable, however, in the health and well-being of a child. If we make an unbalanced investment in medical care to the exclusion of other nonmedical investments, we are either wasting our investment or reducing its full return. Consequently, when addressing children's health, we must focus on an integrated, functional approach that allows children to develop both interdependently and sequentially. *Interdependently* means that a child must develop physically, cognitively, emotionally, and socially. *Sequentially* means that our children grow and learn in stages, with each step built on the previous one. If a child misses an essential developmental step (attachment to his or her parents, the learning of certain gross motor skills, the development of language skills, the knowledge that his or her actions have an effect on others, etc.) other developmental stages are invariably affected.

The lack of an integrated, functional paradigm for children's health has contributed to our society's fragmented

Figure 1.1—The critical components of an Integrated Children's Network.

approach toward its most precious resource—children. The development of a functional paradigm would enable us to focus our attention on the specific needs of children and better integrate and coordinate the services designed to meet those needs. A functional approach to children's health would contribute to a society in which a child is potentially free from disease and disability and can progress normally for his or her age in cognitive and socioemotional development. If we are faithful to such an approach, children will have an opportunity to realize their full potential as healthy, autonomous adults who can contribute their special talents and skills to society.

Our functional model for the delivery of children's services is an Integrated Children's Network (see Figure 1.1). Prevention approaches addressing economic security, medical care, shelter, nutrition, child care, and early education constitute the components of our model. Because each is necessary but cannot stand alone to help a disadvantaged child become an autonomous adult, the Integrated Children's Network takes the form of six interlocking gears. If one of the gears is static or frozen, the child will not have the tools to achieve autonomy.

Economic security is the primary gear in the Integrated Children's Network and the pivotal force of the model. It is essential that a child's economic needs be met if the other gears are to be set in motion. Children lacking economic security will invariably be deprived of the vital services necessary to sustain functional development. Consequently, it is imperative that the children of disadvantaged families receive support.

2 Medical care is the next gear in our functional paradigm. The correlation between economic insecurity and the medically uninsured is easily established. Low-income persons are disproportionately represented among the uninsured. Of the 35 million uninsured Americans, over 10 million are children under 18 years of age.[1] Although children constitute less than one-quarter of the population, they represent nearly 28% of all uninsured Americans.[2]

A large proportion of women lack access to adequate prenatal and postpartum care. It is estimated that close to 25% of US women in their prime childbearing years (15–24) lack a financial source of health care.[3] "Preventing Low Birthweight," a benchmark report released by the Institute of Medicine, highlighted monetary (and other) obstacles women face in obtaining prenatal care.[4] Numerous studies document the marked benefits of adequate prenatal care and its impact on the birth of healthy infants. It is hard to believe that this dimension of medical care has been grossly neglected by society.

3 Shelter is an essential dimension in the development of a child. The destitution of the woman and infant described in the introduction is a reality faced by many children each day in the United States. Through the 1980s, the homeless population shifted away from the historical stereotypes of alcoholics, drug addicts, and transients to a growing number of younger people, including women and children.[5] In fact, the United States Conference of Mayors estimates that families with children constitute 32% of the homeless population.[6] The National Academy of Sciences released a report estimating that 100,000 US children fall asleep homeless every night.[7]

4 Proper nutrition is necessary for the functional development of a child. But hunger has once again become a cause of concern in the United States. Although hunger is not as ubiquitous as it was in the Great Depression or even in the early 1960s, our food shelves and soup kitchens are busy. The use of these "temporary" facilities—which are generally the voluntary efforts of churches, shelters, community groups, and charitable organizations—has increased annually throughout the 1980s. In Minnesota, for example, the use of "emergency" food shelves increased 300% during the 1980s.[8]

Child care is crucial for the children of working families because of economic pressures and tenuous job security. Because 54% of mothers in the out-of-home labor force have infants less than one year of age, the United States must enact cohesive child care legislation and a more progressive maternal-leave policy.[9] Although the maternity leave bill signed by President Clinton is a victory for working mothers, it is only a first step and still falls far short of other Western countries.

5 Early education is the final component of our functional model. A quality early education is necessary for a child to fulfill his or her potential as a productive member of society. It has been demonstrated that quality early education for disadvantaged children improves their lives significantly on many levels. Early education enhances physical health, self-image, focus on the future, parental assistance, linguistic capabilities, and college enrollment.

In this chapter we have given a brief overview of the six components of the Integrated Children's Network. We have introduced the lack of integration and effectiveness of present-day children's services. In the following chapters, we will examine the status of the six components, dedicating a chapter to each. Our inquiry will focus on how each component affects a child's physical, cognitive, and socioemotional development. After we have elaborated on each component of the Integrated Children's Network, we will offer a series of recommendations based on our model. In conclusion, we will offer an ethical commentary that addresses every child's right to possess the tools required to become an autonomous adult.

References

1. *An EBRI Special Report.* Washington, DC: Employee Benefit Research Institute; February 1992:32.

2. Ibid., 30.

3. Gold RB, Kenney AM, Songh S. Paying for maternity care in the United States. *Family Plan Perspective.* 1987; 19:190.

4. Institute of Medicine. *Preventing Low Birthweight.* Washington, DC: National Academy Press; 1985:153.

5. *Homeless—A Complex Problem and the Federal Response.* Washington, DC: US General Accounting Office; 1986.

6. *A Status Report on Hunger and Homelessness in America's Cities: 1992.* Washington, DC: US Conference of Mayors; 1992:2.

7. *Homeless, Health and Human Needs.* Washington, DC: Institute of Medicine; 1988:13–14.

8. *Homegrown Hunger—A Study of People Who Use Emergency Food Shelves in Minnesota.* Minneapolis, Minn: Minnesota Food Education and Resource Center; December 1985.

9. Zigler E, Gillman E. Day care in America: What is needed? *Pediatrics.* 1993; 1:175.

Poverty and the Invisible Child

What does it mean to be poor? There is no denying the impoverishment of the woman and child in front of the Plaza Hotel, but for other Americans and their families, the answer may not be as obvious. The official US poverty standards were developed in the early 1960s by Molly Orshansky to facilitate the collection of information and its eventual analysis and dissemination. Ms Orshansky was a staff member at the research and statistics office of the Social Security Administration. Her formula was based on information obtained from food and income data during the mid-1950s. After examining the Department of Agriculure's economic food plans, she found that expenditures for food represented approximately one-third of a family's income in 1955. Thus, the poverty threshold was derived by simply multiplying this minimum food budget by a factor of three.[1] The poverty level is indexed annually to keep pace with inflation. In 1992, the poverty threshold was $7,143 for a single person and $14,335 for a family of four.[2]

The poverty rate for selected age groups has changed substantially over the past three decades. In 1959, the largest segment of the poor were the elderly. At that time 35%—or over 5 million—were poor. Since then, there has been a significant reduction in the number of elderly persons living in poverty. Their poverty rate is presently at 12.9%, which is slightly less than the overall national poverty rate. The poverty rate for younger adults—between 18 and 64 years of age—has also decreased slightly over the past three decades. Since 1980, however, children were increasingly represented among the poor. In fact, 21.9% of US children live in poverty, and they account for 40% of Americans living below the poverty threshold.[3] Figure 2.1 depicts their increasing poverty rates.

The graph represents the overall poverty rate in the United States from 1959 to 1992 for both children and the

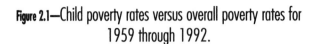

Figure 2.1—Child poverty rates versus overall poverty rates for 1959 through 1992.

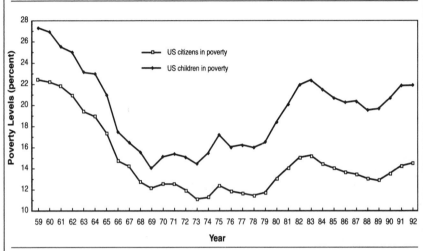

Source: U.S. Bureau of the Census, Current Population Reports, Series P-60, No. 185 "Poverty in the United States 1992", U.S. Government Printing Office, Washington, DC 1993.

general population. There have been three distinct periods in poverty trends. The nation made steady progress in reducing the number of Americans living in poverty during the War on Poverty, which ended in 1968. The next 12 years—from 1968 through 1980—are best characterized as an era of indifference. The United States was diverted from the problems of poverty because it focused on Vietnam, Watergate, and the Iranian hostage crisis. The country was plagued by stagflation, which is an increase in inflation and a decrease in employment. Given the country's economic woes, modest increases in expen-

ditures for social programs were rapidly consumed by inflation. The overall poverty rate during this period remained constant except for minor fluctuations. The minor fluctuations, however, centered around children; consequently, the poverty rates for children started their slow but steady divergence away from the general population.

Since 1980, the primary national political agenda was threefold. First, increased expenditures for defense and national security. The defense budget underwent a $1.7 trillion increase during the 1980s.[4] The second major objective was a reduction of taxes. The Economic

Recovery Tax Act (ERTA) of 1981 enacted major tax reductions that ultimately deprived the government of billions of dollars from 1982 to 1992. Balancing the budget was the third objective.

Recent economic policies have created severe fiscal problems. In 1980, the national debt increased to $994 billion. In 1992, the national debt exploded to over $4 trillion.[5] The United States has become the world's largest debtor nation. The fastest growing dimension of the national budget in 1992 was the $201 billion interest payment on the national debt.[6]

Inability to balance the budget presents a major obstacle to social policy. If the defense budget is increased and the tax base is reduced, funds for social programs will invariably be diminished. The expenditures for entitlement programs such as Social Security and Medicare are politically difficult to cut. These entitlements do not require an annual authorization of federal expenditures. In other words, the federal government is legally obligated to make the required appropriations for persons deemed eligible for Social Security and Medicare.

In addition to Social Security and Medicare, there are domestic discretionary programs (i.e., child nutrition programs, housing assistance, Head Start) that provide a safety net for underserved Americans. Although the domestic discretionary programs represent the smallest portion of the budget, they became a target of reductions intended to balance the budget. In 1980, for example, domestic discretionary programs constituted 5.5% of the gross domestic product; by 1990, domestic discretionary programs were 4% of the gross domestic product.[7]

Given these reductions, the 1980s can best be characterized as an era of neglect for our children. The number of children living in poverty exploded, and the programs designed to ameliorate the consequences of poverty were restricted. Consequently, our children fell into a social-welfare safety net that had unraveled. Although the cause of the present status of children is multifactorial and cannot be attributed to a single person, set of policies, or administration, the exacerbated poverty trends among children during this time are clear. Scant effort was made to rectify these problems at the federal level, presumably leaving solutions to state and local governments.

Regional Demographics

In 1992, 14.6 million, or 21.9%, of our children lived below the poverty threshold.[8] Their plight is endemic in our society.[9] Contrary to popular belief, children's poverty is not restricted to urban ghettos; it has seeped into the suburbs and the rural heartland. The poverty rates for children living in urban, suburban, and rural areas are 30.5%, 13.3%, and 22.9%, respectively.[10] Figure 2.2 shows the pervasiveness of children's poverty across the United States.

The urban ghettos of Chicago, Boston, New York, Detroit, Los Angeles,

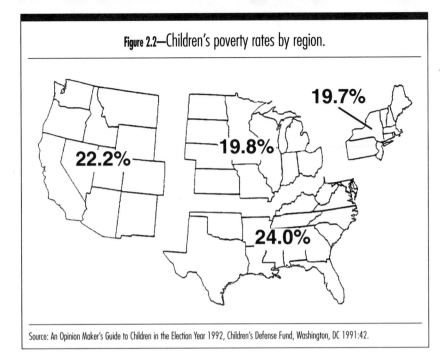

Figure 2.2—Children's poverty rates by region.

19.7%

19.8%

22.2%

24.0%

Source: An Opinion Maker's Guide to Children in the Election Year 1992, Children's Defense Fund, Washington, DC 1991:42.

and other cities are home to many impoverished children who are isolated and hidden from view. They live in projects that serve merely as prisons of oppression, offering little hope of escape. Washington, DC, epitomizes the plight of the urban poor. Our nation's capital is graced by monuments to Washington, Lincoln, and Jefferson. The White House radiates an air of majesty, but two blocks away the "other" Washington begins. The blocks of row houses where people attempt to survive from day to day are hidden from the tourists and the upwardly mobile workers commuting into the city on the multimillion-dollar rail system known as the Metro. The proposed Metro line through the city's poorest quadrant, Southeast Washington, has never been initiated, and another line skirts the edges of Northeast Washington, forgoing stops in the poorest sections of the town.

For Black Americans, poverty remains hidden in rural counties and inner-city slums. In 1985, the *Washington Post* printed an article entitled, "Rural Blacks Live in Poverty."[11] The article highlighted the problems in Northern Worcester County on Maryland's eastern shore. Ocean City, part of Worcester County, is known for miles of rolling seashore and the tens of thousands of visitors who besiege the town on sweltering summer days. But this was not the experience of Myron Joyner, a 10-year-old Black boy who lived with his mother in a two-room shack made of composition board, cinder blocks, and tin. Myron's mother spoke bluntly of their existence: "It's not fit for human beings around here. But if they close these houses down, we really would have no place to go, no place to rent. Not poor Black people anyway."[12]

In the lower Rio Grande Valley of Texas, 250,000 Americans live in more than 400 rural slums known as *colonias*, which are unincorporated rural subdivisions of earth dotted by makeshift shacks. These dwellings lack heat, water, and adequate sewage systems. The water supply of the *colonias* is contaminated, and chronic disease runs rampant. In its examination of the *colonias*, *Newsweek* reported on the plight of the Costilla family. Gloria Costilla, her husband, and their eight children lived in a two-room home with dirt floors. Because the family was unable to afford either a $200 meter installation fee or a monthly water supply fee, Gloria Costilla rose each morning and retrieved eight 10-gallon buckets of water from a neighbor's house. Iris Hernandez, executive director of the Hidalgo County Health Care Corporation, had a poignant synopsis of the *colonias:* "It's like we live in a forgotten land down here."[13]

Racial Composition and Feminization of Children's Poverty

Race and ethnic background are determining factors in a person's economic status. Minority children have been disproportionately represented among the poor. Significant economic improvement was made by all children during the 1960s. Poverty rates for White children were cut in half from 1959 to 1969.[14] The poverty rate for Black children declined from over 65% in 1959 to a low of 39.6% in 1969.[15] (Data were not available for Hispanic children until 1973.)

Progress by the War on Poverty was eroded in the 1980s. Nearly half of all Black children, or 4.7 million, are living in poverty. They constitute 33.1% of the total number of children living below the poverty threshold.[16] The number of Hispanic children living in poverty reached 3 million in 1991, which represents 21.5% of all children living in poverty.[17] Although Black and Hispanic children constitute only 27.3% of the population under 18, they represent 54.6% of the children living below the poverty threshold.[18]

One must examine family composition when investigating the problem of children in poverty, because it is one of the most potent determinants of poverty. The percentage of children living in female-headed, single-parent families has increased substantially since 1959, when only 8.8% of children lived in these households. At present, single females head 54% of all American families below the poverty threshold.[19] Seventy-eight percent of Black and 46% of Hispanic families living in poverty are headed by a single female.[20]

The *feminization of poverty* is a phrase that has been used more often in our culture over the last decade. The phrase encompasses a variety of social and economic trends that have resulted in an inordinate number of female-headed households living below the poverty threshold. Ruth Sidel, in *Women and Children Last: The Plight of Poor Women in Affluent America,* addressed the various factors leading to the present impoverishment of women and, consequently, their children[21]:

Table 2.1
Relative Frequency of Medical Problems among Low-Income and Other Children

Health Problem	Relative Frequency in Low-Income Children
Low birthweight	Twofold
Delayed immunization	Threefold
Asthma	More prevalent
Bacterial meningitis	Twofold
Rheumatic fever	Two-and-a-half times
Lead poisoning	Threefold
Neonatal mortality	One-and-a-half times
Postneonatal mortality	Twofold to threefold
Deaths due to accidents	Twofold to threefold
Deaths due to disease	Threefold to fourfold
Complications of appendicitis	Twofold to threefold
Diabetic ketoacidosis	Twofold
Severely impaired vision	Twofold
Severe iron-deficiency anemia	Twofold

Source: B. Starfield. *Effectiveness of Medical Care: Validating Clinical Wisdom*, Baltimore: Johns Hopkins University Press; 1985.

■ The weakening of the traditional nuclear family;

■ The rapid growth in female-headed, single-parent families;

■ A labor market that discriminates actively against female workers;

■ A welfare system that seeks to maintain its recipients below the poverty level;

■ The time-consuming but unpaid domestic responsibilities of women, particularly child care; and

■ Nationwide pressure to dismantle programs designed to serve those most in need.

Medical Consequences

Preterm gestation can result in low birth weight, respiratory distress syndrome

(RDS), and sudden infant death syndrome (SIDS): major causes of death in the first year of life. Because these conditions are predominant among infants born to impoverished mothers, the infant mortality rate of the poor is significantly higher than that of the general populace.[22] The infant mortality rates for White and Black children in the United States reflect this fact. In 1990, the infant mortality rate for White infants was 7.6 deaths per 1000 live births; for Black infants, it was 18.0, which is on a par with a number of Third World countries.[23]

Because of poor families' inability to secure the appropriate medical services for their children, poor children utilize Health care services far less often than middle-class children.[24] Numerous studies have demonstrated that poor children are less likely to have a regular source of medical care or to receive preventive health care.[25] Consequently, as poor infants progress into childhood, they are faced with many health care obstacles. Table 2.1 compares the relative frequency of medical problems in low-income and other children.[26]

Cognitive and Developmental Consequences

Children from poor socioeconomic backgrounds are plagued by academic underachievement, grade retention, and special education placement.[27] The medical complications of poverty such as low birthweight, anemia, lead poisoning, and so on, impair physical as well as cognitive development. An infant with organic brain damage caused by untreated lead poisoning or fetal alcohol syndrome is cognitively impaired before he or she reaches first grade.

Psychosocial and emotional factors hinder the cognitive and developmental progress of poor children. Greg Duncan of the University of Michigan found that children who were born with low birthweights and suffered from continuous poverty during their first 5 years of life have IQs that are 9.1 points lower than children never subjected to poverty.[28] A 1988 study conducted by Zill and Schoenborn uncovered a correlation among income, mental health, and learning disabilities. The study found that children living in families whose annual income was below $10,000 had a 25% higher rate of emotional and behavioral problems than their counterparts from families with annual incomes over $40,000.[29] The Zill and Schoenborn study also revealed that the frequency of learning disabilities for children living in the lower socioeconomic strata is approximately 40% greater than those from the higher socioeconomic strata.[30] The National Longitudinal Survey of Young Americans disclosed that over half the children between 15 and 18 years of age living below the poverty threshold are situated in the lowest 20th percentile in reading and math skills for their respective ages.[31]

Although there is a large gap in the educational achievement of White and Black children, poor children, regardless of race, are three times as likely to drop out of high school as middle-class children.[32] The overwhelming dropout rate of poor children can be linked to causes other than medical and emotional complications. The parents of many poor children have not graduated from high school.[33] Although the parents of poor children want to see their children receive a high school diploma, they may not have the personal or economic resources to further their children's education. Given the learning deficits and other educational problems of impoverished children, it is imperative that they receive the highest quality teachers, low student-to-teacher ratios, and the finest facilities if they are to excel. Unfortunately, this is not the reality. It is common for expenditures per student in affluent school districts to be twice that of expenditures in disadvantaged school districts.[34]

Because of the early medical, cognitive, and socioemotional obstacles for poor children, dropping out of high school is associated with many other developmental problems. Researchers have found strong links between an inability to complete high school, increased juvenile delinquency, teenage pregnancy, and intergenerational economic dependency.[35]

Children's Poverty and the Government's Response

The Social Security Act of 1935, enacted over 50 years ago, was the federal government's attempt to provide a minimum level of subsistence for those in need. In 1935, as today, the elderly, disabled, and children were the three most vulnerable groups. Title II of the Social Security Act of 1935, or the Old Age Survivor and Disability Insurance (OASDI), is commonly referred to as Social Security, which is financed through payroll deductions (FICA, or Federal Insurance Contributions Act). After contributing to the system for 10 years, an individual and spouse are entitled to draw a monthly federal pension upon retirement. The monthly pension is based on a person's yearly earnings while he or she was in the workforce. Because there are no income or asset requirements to be met before a person is eligible, OASDI is a non–means-tested entitlement program.

Title IV, another income support program in the Social Security Act of 1935, was originally called Aid to Dependent Children (ADC). The roots of the ADC program were entrenched in the ideology that distinguished the "deserving" poor from the "undeserving" poor. The program supplemented the needs of only the "deserving" poor because it was thought that their destitution was beyond their control. In 1950, however, the act was amended to allow additional cash assistance for the mother (parent) responsible for raising the child or children. After 1950, the ADC program was transformed into Aid to Families with Dependent Children (AFDC), or what is commonly called welfare.[36]

The AFDC program is fundamentally different from OASDI. AFDC is not solely a federal program but a federal-state partnership. Federal grants are made to the states, and the states are given considerable latitude in setting income thresholds and other eligibility standards for the AFDC program. AFDC is a means-tested entitlement, which means that a family has to meet a basic income eligibility standard to qualify for the program. Each state sets its own "standard of need" by calculating a minimum level of subsistence required by an individual or family in that particular state. The states are not obligated, however, to grant this amount to recipients and, in many cases, the amount is substantially less than the standard of need that has actually been calculated. The AFDC program provides cash subsidies to needy children (and their caretakers) who lack adequate financial support because at least one parent is dead, disabled, and/or continually absent from the home. All 50 states, the District of Columbia, Guam, Puerto Rico, and the Virgin Islands offer AFDC for one-parent families. Prior to 1988, 23 states offered AFDC for two-parent poor families if the main breadwinner was unemployed.[37] Because of the AFDC–Unemployed Parents (AFDC–UP) legislation of 1991, the states are mandated to provide assistance for two-parent families in which the principal wage earner is unemployed.[38] The states are required to provide AFDC–UP benefits only for six months.[39]

AFDC and OASDI programs have fared differently over the years. The elderly have made tremendous progress at reducing their poverty rates, while children have suffered from escalating poverty. OASDI has experienced a political and fiscal affirmation from Congress over the years in the form of frequent increases in Social Security payments. In 1972, Congress amended the OASDI program by creating an automatic cost of living adjustment (COLA), which indexes Social Security payments to keep pace with inflation and ensures that the purchasing power of the elderly is not eroded by inflation.

State payments to AFDC recipients are often inequitable. Not one state distributes AFDC payments equal to the poverty threshold.[40] Alaska is the only state that grants an AFDC payment between 75% and 100% of the poverty threshold.[41] The AFDC payments of 38 states fall below 50% of the poverty threshold.[42] In Mississippi, for example, the cash allotment for a family of four is $144 a month.[43] Only 15 states grant AFDC recipients monthly payments that the respective state has calculated to be a minimum standard of need.[44]

The beginning of these AFDC payment reductions can be traced to the enactment of the Omnibus Budget Reconciliation Act of 1981 (OBRA 81). OBRA 81 realigned federal and state responsibilities and orchestrated a major reduction in social support programs. Because of changes in eligibility criteria for the Work Incentive Program (WIN)—part of the AFDC program—442,000 families were eliminated from the AFDC program. The 442,000 families affected by the OBRA legislation were left without cash assistance, child care, and access to health services through the Medicaid program.[45] Because of the OBRA 81 legislation and the other AFDC cuts through the 1980s, nearly half the families living in poverty are ineligible for assistance. Those families who are eligible have experienced a reduction in their cash assistance and other necessary services. Is it any wonder that we are witnessing a growing number of families with children living on the edge?

Certain myths, which harken back to the idea of the deserving and undeserving poor, have arisen to justify the federal government's destructive AFDC policies. A popular view maintains that AFDC invariably engenders lifelong and intergenerational dependency for its recipients. Given the fact that the median length of AFDC assistance is only 23 months, it is difficult to imagine why this myth has been given such credence.[46] Thirty-four percent of AFDC recipients are on the rolls for a year or less, and 53% are on the rolls for two years or less.[47] Another prevalent myth is that AFDC recipients have many children. The reality is that the average adult AFDC recipient has 1.9 children.[48] Our children deserve something better than public policy that is driven by myths and disinformation.

References

1. Murray C. *Losing Ground: American Social Policy 1950–1980*. New York: Basic Books, Inc.; 1984:271.

2. *Poverty in the United States: 1992*. Washington, DC: US Bureau of the Census; 1993: Table A-8. Current Population Reports, P-60 ser., no. 185.

3. Ibid., Table 3.

4. *Statistical Abstract of the United States: 1992*. Washington, DC: US Bureau of the Census; 1992:315.

5. *The Economic and Budget Outlook: Fiscal Years 1994-1998*. Washington, DC: Congressional Budget Office; 1993:57.

6. *An Analysis of the President's Budgetary Proposal for Fiscal Year 1993*. Washington, DC: Congressional Budget Office; March 1992:128.

7. *The Economic and Budget Outlook: Fiscal Years 1993–1997*. Washington, DC: Congressional Budget Office; 1992:51.

8. *Poverty in the United States:1992*. Washington, DC: US Bureau of the Census: 1993. Table 3. Current Population Reports, P-60 ser., no. 185.

9. *An Opinion Maker's Guide to Children in the Election Year 1992: Leave No Child Behind*. Washington, DC: Children's Defense Fund; 1991:41.

10. Ibid., 42.

11. Pressley SA, "Near Ocean City's condos, rural Blacks live in poverty." *Washington Post*, July 28, 1985.

12. Ibid.

13. Gibney F. "In Texas, a grim new Appalachia lives in the nation's poorest region." *Newsweek*, June 8, 1987:27–28.

14. *Poverty in the United States: 1991*. Washington, DC: US Bureau of the Census; 1992: Table 3. Current Population Reports, Series P-60, no. 181.

15. Ibid.

16. Ibid.

17. Ibid.

18. Ibid.

19. Ibid.

20. Ibid.

21. Sidel R. *Women and Children Last—The Plight of Poor Women in Affluent America.* New York: Penguin; 1987, 1-30.

22. Klerman LV. *Children in Poverty.* New York: Cambridge University Press; 1991:138.

23. Advance Report of Final Mortality Statistics 1990. *Monthly Vital Statistics* Report. 1993; 41(7).

24. *Children in Poverty.* Klerman LV. New York: Cambridge University Press; 1991:144.

25. Ibid.

26. Starfield B. Child and adolescent health status measure. *The Future of Children.* 1992; 2(2):33.

27. Ibid., 190.

28. Duncan G, Brooks-Gunn J, Klebanov P. Economic deprivation and early childhood development. *Childhood Development* (Special Issue: Children and Poverty), 65 (2), 1994:307.

29. Klerman LV. The health of poor children: Problems and programs. In: A Huston, ed. *Children in Poverty.* New York, NY: Cambridge University Press; 1991:140.

30. Ibid., 140.

31. Zill N, Scoenborn C. *The Health of Our Nation's Children: Developmental, Learning and Emotional Problems, 1988 Advance Data.* Publication No. 190. Hyattsville, Maryland. National Center for Health Statistics, 1990:7.

32. Ibid.

33. Ibid., 73.

34. Ibid., 73.

35. Klerman LV. *The health of poor children: Problems and programs.* In: A Huston, ed. *Children in Poverty.* New York: Cambridge University Press; 1991:190.

36. *Background Material and Data on Programs within the Jurisdiction of the Committee on Ways and Means.* Washington, DC: U.S. House of Representatives Committee; 1989 ed:517. Print WMCP 101-4.

37. Ibid., 533.

38. *Overview of Entitlements: 1992 Green Book.* Washington, DC: Committee on Ways and Means, U.S. House of Representatives; 1992:603.

39. Ibid.

40. Fax from Adminstration for Children and Families, September 1992.

41. Ibid.

42. *Green Book: Overview of Entitlement Programs,* Washington, DC: US House of Representatives, Committee on Ways and Means; 1992.

43. Ibid.

44. Ibid.

45. *An Evaluation of the 1981 AFDC Changes: Initial Analysis.* Washington, DC: General Accounting Office; 1984. Pub. No. GAO/pemb-84-6.

46. Administration of Children and Families, *Characteristics and Financial Circumstances of AFDC Recipients.* Washington, DC: US Department of Health and Human Services; 1992:1.

47. Ibid.

CHAPTER THREE

The Uninsured and Unprotected

> " Of all forms of inequity, injustice in health care is the most shocking and the most inhumane."
>
> —**MARTIN LUTHER KING, JR.**

During the 1990s, we will face an alarming escalation of health care costs. In 1993, for example, health care expenditures of $940 billion, or 14% of the gross national product (GNP), were projected.[1] Despite the spiraling escalation of health care expenditures, an ever-increasing proportion of Americans lack access to adequate health care services. A recent estimate of the "uninsured" population exceeds 35.7 million persons, or more than 16.6% of our general population.[2] If the underinsured are included, the National Center for Health Services Research (NCHSR) estimates that 50 million individuals—or nearly one-quarter of our population—are inadequately protected against the possibility of a catastrophic illness.[3] It seems inconceivable that a nation spending over $2.5 billion a day on health care services would have such a large population lacking access to health care.

The age distribution of the uninsured is the most noticeable statistic. Children under 18 years of age constitute 9.8 million, or 27.5 %, of the uninsured.[4] The children of the working or corridor poor (families whose incomes are between 100% and 200% of the poverty level) account for 36% of uninsured children.[5]

The fact that our society neglects expectant mothers and their unborn children is another grave social injustice. Conception to birth is the most critical period in the development of a child. Numerous studies have documented the marked benefits of prenatal care and its impact on the birth of healthy infants. The correlation between negative birth outcomes and inadequate prenatal care is irrefutable. Yet access to comprehensive prenatal care is threatened for a large percentage of women. In 1991, 21% of all women in their prime childbearing years (ages 18 through 29) lacked financial access to health care.[6] "Blessed Events and the Bottom Line," a major report released in 1987, underscored monetary concerns as a decisive factor for women who did not seek prenatal care.[7]

Employment and Health Care

Because low-income persons are disproportionately represented among the uninsured, the interplay between poverty and lack of insurance is easily established. But this relationship is not direct by any means. Prior to the passage of Medicare and Medicaid in 1965, a family's access to health insurance was best characterized by its income. Today, however, we are faced with a different trend. Americans living on the extremes of the financial spectrum have been assured health care services. For the most part, the poorest of the poor—the families living well below the poverty threshold—are covered by Medicaid. Families of the middle and upper financial strata have either employer-subsidized health care plans or individually financed health coverage. Consequently, the corridor poor represent an ever-increasing proportion of families who lack access to adequate health care.

Given unemployment, underemployment, self-employment, or seasonal work, many of the corridor poor fail to receive employer-paid coverage. The corridor poor are generally unable to purchase health care coverage for themselves or their families, and the vast majority of them fail to meet the strict eligibility criteria of Medicaid or other public sources of health care. Roughly 54% of the uninsured in the United States live in families where the household head is employed full-time.[8]

Since insurance companies have a tendency to charge small firms (those employing 25 workers or less) higher premiums, many small businesses cannot afford to obtain health insurance for their employees. Consequently, 29% of employees in small firms are uninsured.[9] The proliferating number of low-income, service-sector jobs and the practice of hiring part-time employees who do not work enough hours a week to qualify for benefits have denied millions of Americans health insurance.

A University of Michigan study found that 51% of the unemployed in the Detroit area had lost their employer-based coverage and were unable to obtain a public or private form of health insurance.[10] Although the employer-based plan may allow for a continuation of the group plan or even a conversion of the company's group rate to an individual rate, the unemployed individual is faced with the dilemma of financing the entire cost of the premium at a time when he or she is already financially restricted. Given these and other factors, the number of uninsured Americans has risen by more than 11 million since 1980.[11] It is painfully clear that the problem of the uninsured is not only one of poverty or income, but, ironically, one of employment.

The No Card, No Care Syndrome

Millions of American families are forced to play the health care gamble. They must choose between their immediate needs of survival (housing, food, transportation, etc.) and their less apparent need for health care protection. When a family living on the edge must choose between feeding hungry children or purchasing health care insurance, the choice seems obvious. The lack of health insurance ultimately places the lives of their children at the most risk when they face a medical emergency.

The first two questions most commonly asked of a person entering a doctor's office, clinic, or hospital are "What is the name of your insurance company?" and "May I see your card?" A provider card furnished by insurers unlocks the health care door for the majority of Americans. The provider card may be furnished by a traditional insurance company like Blue Cross/Blue Shield, an HMO, or Medicaid. Although many providers do not accept Medical Assistance, Medicaid's card unlocks a few health care doors—albeit back doors. The no card, no care syndrome invariably produces situations like the following for uninsured parents.

Ginger was in tears. Her husband, David, a contract laborer, had his arm around her. He was close to tears himself. The doctor had just disclosed to Ginger and David that their newborn, Jonathan, born 5 weeks premature and at a low birthweight, was severely jaundiced. His bilirubin level was 18.4—a bilirubin level of 20 may cause irreversible brain damage. David and Ginger didn't have health insurance and they didn't have the money to

pay for Jonathan's re-hospitalization. Against their doctor's wishes, David and Ginger brought Jonathan home and rented special lights. The couple stayed up 24 hours a day for 5 days to keep the infant immersed in the light. Ginger and David were extremely lucky, because Jonathan managed to survive. "We know we took a dangerous risk, but we felt we had no other choice," Ginger said of her trauma. "When we found out I was pregnant we were upset because we knew we weren't financially able to care for a child. But our religious convictions left us no alternative but to do the best we could."[12]

The no card, no care syndrome has also engendered patient dumping: transferring patients in need of emergency services from one hospital to another because the patients do not have a source of payment. Patients are frequently transferred from private and proprietary hospitals to public and teaching hospitals. Information on patient dumping is limited because it is not the type of practice that an institution wants to discuss. To address this problem, the Consolidated Omnibus Budget Reconciliation Act (COBRA) of 1985 required that a patient be stabilized before being transferred.[13] Patient dumping, however, is a common practice.[14] A study of Cook County Hospital in Chicago revealed that the practice of patient dumping has an insidious price: the study found higher mortality rates for transferred patients than for nontransferred patients with a comparable illness.[15] The following anecdote demonstrates how patient dumping endangers the lives of infants.

A pediatrician in a Rock Hill, South Carolina hospital attempts to transfer a comatose 3-year-old girl to a better equipped urban medical center. But, because her family has no health insurance, two hospitals in close proximity refuse to take her. Finally, a hospital 100 miles away accepts the child.[16]

Preadmission deposits, another product of the no card, no care syndrome, are designed to weed out those who cannot afford medical care. The uninsured person is required to furnish a deposit prior to entry into the hospital or clinic. If the deposit is not paid, the person is denied admission. This practice has had a severe impact on obstetric and pediatric care.

A public clinic refers a desperately ill baby to a regional medical center for treatment. The baby's parents are indigent and do not possess a preadmission deposit. After waiting in the medical center's emergency room for four hours, the baby is finally admitted by a radiologist. Because the pediatrician on call did not want to serve as a backup for a "free clinic," he refused to treat the baby.[17]

The no card, no care syndrome hits public hospitals much harder than private hospitals because public hospitals generally accept the uninsured. In 1991, uncompensated hospital care—charity care and bad debt—totaled $13.4 billion.[18] Although public hospitals account for less than a quarter of all hospital care, they assume nearly a third of all uncompensated care.[19] Hospitals in the midst of financial instability have a tendency to minimize their uncompensated care by reducing certain services. The services affecting families and children—for example, prenatal and maternity care, newborn intensive care units (NICUs), and outpatient ambulatory care—account for most of the uncompensated care.

The Impact of Uninsured Mothers and Children

A large percentage of women in their prime childbearing years lack insurance. Whereas the uninsured rate for the general population is 17%, it is 59% for women aged 15 to 19 years of age and 33% for women between 20 and 24 years of age.[20] Consequently, only 75.5% of mothers in the United States received prenatal care in their first trimester.[21] Although the infant mortality rate for the United States has improved throughout the 1980s, it is still unacceptably high, especially for minorities.[22] One study found that uninsured Black newborns have four times greater risk of adverse hospital outcomes than insured White newborns.[23]

Low birthweight can be a direct consequence of inadequate prenatal care. In 1980 6.8% of infants born in the United States suffered from low birthweight and by 1991 the percentage increased to 7.1.[24] An infant born at a low birthweight is almost 40 times more likely to die in the first month of life than an infant born at a normal weight.[25] Nearly 66% of all infant deaths are attributable to low birthweight.[26] In addition to infant mortality, low birthweight produces birth defects, mental retardation, seizure disorders, and cerebral palsy.[27] The Department of Health and Human Services estimates that 80% of the women at risk of having low-birthweight babies are identifiable during their first prenatal visit, at which time an intervention can be initiated.[28]

Medically uninsured children face formidable barriers to health care. A National Medical Care Utilization and Expenditure Survey revealed that insured children average 1.3 more physician visits than uninsured children and accrue more than twice the medical charges.[29] The health care disparities alluded to by the National Medical Care Utilization and Expenditure Survey range from preventive care to ambulatory visits.

There is a large disparity between insured and uninsured children in the use of ambulatory health care services, which include all physician contacts except inpatient. The 1987 National Medical Expenditure Survey found that 80% of insured children had ambulatory contact, compared with 60% of uninsured children.[30] Whereas 90% of insured children under the age of 5 had at least one ambulatory visit, only 75% of their uninsured counterparts had an ambulatory visit.[31]

Because of the lack of insurance and other barriers to adequate health care, over 40% of children between the ages of 1 and 4 have not received immunizations against common childhood diseases, which include measles, mumps, rubella, polio, diphtheria, pertussis, and tetanus.[32] Forgoing immunizations can be devastating. Their immense cost savings in the long run means that every child in the United States should receive basic vaccinations.

A study by Stoddard et al. reveals the harmful repercussions of the lack of insurance for children. The authors examined 7578 children whose ages ranged from 1 to 17 years. They compared the incidence of pharyngitis/tonsillitis, acute ear infections, recurrent ear infections, and asthma between uninsured and insured children who went without a physician visit. Compared with uninsured children, insured children suffering from pharyngitis/tonsillitis, acute ear infections, recurrent ear infections, and asthma were 51%, 53%, 120%, and 43%, respectively, more likely to visit a physician for their maladies.[33] The ramifications of these lopsided percentages are alarming. Pharyngitis may lead to peritonsillar and retropharyngeal abscess, acute glomerulonephritis, or rheumatic fever, which may cause permanent debilitation or even death. If a middle-ear infection is untreated, it can produce hearing loss and speech and language disorders. Untreated asthma can cause respiratory failure and death.

Prescription drugs are extremely important to the pediatric and adolescent population for acute childhood illnesses like strep throat and staph infections, as well as more chronic conditions like asthma and allergies. The disparity in their use between insured and uninsured children is extremely disheartening. The 1987 National Medical Expenditure found that only 34% of children who were uninsured year-round used prescription drugs, compared with 55% of their insured counterparts.[34]

In this section we have looked at the medical neglect of our children. Because there are millions of uninsured children suffering from untreated conditions, we have only scratched the surface. The following data, supplied by the Children's Defense Fund, provides an insight into the *daily* pervasiveness of the problem.[35]

- 1340 babies are born to teenage mothers.
- 638 babies are born to mothers who have received late prenatal care or none at all.
- 742 babies are born at a low birthweight.
- 107 infants die before their first birthday.
- 2 children under the age of 5 are murdered.

Cognitive and Socioemotional Impact of Uninsured Children

The medical, cognitive, and socioemotional consequences suffered by unin-sured children are interrelated, self-evident, and lack definitive demarcations. Infant mortality that is the product of inadequate prenatal care, which in turn is a product of a lack of insurance, is probably the most blatant example. Birth defects, mental retardation, seizure disorders, and cerebral palsy caused by low birthweight have a profound effect on a child's development.

Major developmental consequences may arise if a child does not receive basic immunizations from measles, mumps, rubella, polio, diphtheria, pertussis, tetanus, and so on. Polio, diphtheria, and tetanus can produce irreversible brain damage, which in turn can affect cognitive and sensory motor development.

The disparity in ambulatory visits between insured and uninsured children can translate into thwarted cognitive and socioemotional development, even though it might not be apparent initially. The study by Stoddard et al. proves this point. Peritonsillar and retropharyngeal abscess, acute glomerulonephritis, and rheumatic fever caused by untreated pharyngitis may cause permanent brain damage. The hearing loss and speech and language disorders produced by untreated ear infections will affect school performance and, consequently, socioemotional development.

The disparity in the use of prescription drugs between insured and uninsured children is another source of cognitive and socioemotional differences. If children with diabetes and seizure disorders do not receive proper medication, their cognitive and socioemotional development can be arrested. Conditions such as strep throat and bacterial meningitis, if left untreated by antibiotics, can produce severe physical complications that affect cognitive and socioemotional development.

Uninsured Mothers and Children and the Federal Response

When discussing the issue of uninsured children, we must also discuss Title XIX of the Social Security Amendments of 1965, or Medicaid, which was created to provide financial access to health care for low-income Americans. Medicaid, enacted during the 89th Congress of the United States, mandated the creation of a jointly funded federal-state partnership to help eliminate the financial barriers that low-income children and other Americans faced when attempting to gain access to health care.

The federal government's grants for Medicaid match each state's expenditures, which are based on a formula that takes into account the state's per capita income and range from approximately 50% to 75% of the state's Medicaid budget. Medicaid's primary purpose was to consolidate several different grant programs that were administered by the states. Initially, Medicaid was supposed to add only $250 million to the health care expenditures of the federal government.[36] In Medicaid's first year of operation, however, the combined federal and state outlays were $1.5 billion.

Medicaid underwent tremendous growth during its first decade in both expenditures and in the number of participants. In 1966, 26 states had operating Medicaid programs. By 1976, the 48 states participating in the Medicaid program had a total of 22.8 million enrollees and a combined federal and state outlay of $14.2 billion.[37] The benefits provided to Medicaid recipients also increased. In 1967, the Early Periodic Screening Diagnosis and Treatment (EPSDT) program was enacted, guaranteeing preventive services for children receiving Medicaid benefits.

Medicaid was altered, however, with the passage of the Social Security Amendments of 1972, which established and federalized the Supplemental Security Income (SSI) program. The SSI population included the elderly, blind, and disabled. The federal government deemed SSI recipients automatically eligible for Medicaid benefits. Medicaid allocation for the Aid to Families with Dependent Children (AFDC) population, on the other hand, was dictated solely by the individual states' eligibility requirements. The inequities produced by the Social Security Amendments of 1972 had a profound impact on the distribution of Medicaid expenditures between the AFDC and SSI populations.

The Reagan administration enacted the Omnibus Budget Reconciliation Act of 1981 (OBRA 81), which mandated reductions in federal grants to Medicaid for a 3-year period. As discussed in the previous chapter, OBRA 81 cut close to half a million working families—and consequently about 700,000 children—from the Medicaid program.[38]

Because of the Social Security Amendments of 1972 and OBRA 81, a significant shift in Medicaid enrollment and expenditures occurred between the AFDC and SSI populations during the 1980s. The federal government substantially reduced the states' flexibility and discretion in administration of the SSI program. AFDC implementation of Medicaid, however, still varied from state to state. With this departure from its initial vision, Medicaid soon became a major funding source for long-term care, which accounts for the uneven expenditures between the AFDC and SSI populations. In 1972, for example, AFDC children under the age of 21 received only 18% of Medicaid expenditures; their percentage of Medicaid expenditures plummeted to a low of 11.7% by 1984.[39]

To counteract this trend, Congress initiated a series of incremental Medicaid expansions in 1984, beginning with the enactment of the Deficit Reduction Act (DEFRA) of 1984, which contained provisions known as the Child Health Assurance Program. This program expanded Medicaid eligibility to include "Ribicoff children," who did not formerly qualify for Medicaid under the AFDC umbrella. DEFRA was followed by annual Medicaid expansions that included provisions in the Consolidated Omnibus Budget Reconciliation Act (COBRA) of 1985; the Omnibus Budget Reconcilia-

tion Acts (OBRA) of 1986, 1987, and 1989; and the Medicare Catastrophic Reform Act of 1988, which was subsequently repealed *except* for its Medicaid expansion components.[40] Finally, the 101st Congress enacted the Omnibus Budget Reconciliation Act (OBRA) of 1990, which extends eligibility for Medicaid over the next decade to all children under 18 who live below the federal poverty level.[41] In addition to these legislative options, a relatively obscure Medicaid provision grants a state the right to extend coverage to all children under the age of 19 and pregnant women.[42]

Although Medicaid has expanded its eligibility criteria for children, the concomitant equities have failed to materialize. In 1990, AFDC children accounted for 44% of all Medicaid recipients but received only 14% of Medicaid expenditures; whereas the elderly, blind, and disabled accounted for only 27% of the Medicaid population but received 71% of its expenditures.[43] Thirty-five percent of our infants and children under the age of 18 living below the poverty threshold are not covered by Medicaid.[44]

The 1981 Presidential Commission for the Study of Ethical Problems in Medicine stated, "Society has an ethical obligation to ensure equitable access to health care for all."[45] It is painfully apparent that during the 1980s the federal government did not feel ethically obligated to ensure access to health care for our most precious, yet vulnerable resource—our children.

References

1. *Faulkner and Gray's Medicine and Health.* January 1993; 47:1.

2. *An EBRI Special Report.* Washington, DC: The Employee Benefit Research Institute; February 1992:8.

3. Farley P. *Who are the Underinsured.* Rockville, MD: National Health Care Expenditure Study, US Dept of Health and Human Services, 1984.

4. *An EBRI Special Report.* Washington, DC: The Employee Benefit Research Institute; February 1992:9.

5. Ibid., 69.

6. Ibid., 46.

7. *Blessed Events and the Bottom Line.* Washington, DC: The Alan Guttmacher Institute; 1987.

8. *An EBRI Special Report.* Washington, DC: The Employee Benefit Research Institute; February 1992:24.

9. Ibid., 11.

10. Berki S E, et al. Health Insurance coverage of the unemployed. *Medical Care.* 1985; 23:847.

11. Himmelstein D, Woolhandler S. *The National Health Programs Chartbook.* Washington, DC: Center for National Health Program Studies; 1992:4.

12. The Children's Defense Fund—Minnesota Project; 1985.

13. *Patient Dumping After COBRA.* Washington, DC: US Dept of Health and Human Services; Office of the Inspector General; 1988:1-15.

14. Ibid.

15. Schiff R L, et al, Transfers to a Public Hospital—a Prospective Study of 467 Patients. *New England Journal of Medicine.* 1988; 314:552.

16. Hospitals in cost squeeze dump more patients who can't pay bills. *Wall Street Journal,* March 8, 1985:1.

17. Rosenbaum S. Testimony of the Children's Defense Fund Before the National Council on Health Planning and Development on Uncompensated Care in a Competitive Environment—Whose problem is it? October 1984:9.

18. *American Hospital Association Survey Data, 1980-1991,* Chicago: American Hospital Association; 1991:4.

19. Oral communication with Prospective Payment Assessment Commission, Washington, DC, December 1992.

20. Oberg C. Medically uninsured children in the United States: A challenge to public policy. *Pediatrics.* May 1990; 85:825.

21. Ibid.

22. Advance Report of Final Mortality Statistics 1990. *Monthly Vital Statistics Report.* 41, 7. Washington, DC: US Government Printing Office; 1993.

23. Braveman P et al. Adverse outcomes and lack of health insurance among newborns in an eight-county area of California, 1982 to 1986. *New England Journal Medicine.* 1989; 321:508.

24. The State of America's Children—Yearbook 1994. Children's Defense Fund, Washington, DC, 1994:74.

25. Oberg C. Medically uninsured children in the United States: A challenge to public policy. *Pediatrics.* May 1990; 85:827.

26. Ibid.

27. Ibid., 828.

28. Ibid.

29. Ibid.

30. Monheit A, Cunningham P. Children without health insurance. *The Future of Children.* 1992; 2:160.

31. Ibid., 160-161.

32. Baily B. Access to health care in the United States. In: *Caring for the Uninsured and Underinsured*, Chicago: American Medical Association; 1991:104.

33. Stoddard J, St. Peter R, Newacheck P. Impact of insurance status of ambulatory care utilization for selected childhood condition. Presented at the American Public Health Association, Washington, DC, November 10, 1992:9.

34. Monheit A, Cunningham P. Children without health insurance. *The Future of Children.* 1992; 2:162.

35. *An Opinion Maker's Guide to Children in the Election Year 1992: Leave No Child Behind.* Washington, DC: Children's Defense Fund; 1991: Back cover.

36. O'Sullivan J. *Medicaid: Legislative History, Program Description and Major Issues.* Washington, DC: Congressional Research Service; July 1984:6. Report no. 84–140.

37. Oberg C, Polich C. Medicaid: Entering the third decade. *Health Affairs.* Fall 1988:85.

38. *An Evaluation of the 1981 AFDC Changes: Final Report.* Washington, DC: General Accounting Office; July 2, 1985. GAO/PEMD pub. no. 85–4.

39. Oberg C, Polich C. Medicaid: Entering the third decade. *Health Affairs.* Fall 1988:88.

40. Oberg C. Medically uninsured children in the United States: A challenge to public policy. *Pediatrics.* 1990; 85:824-833.

41. The Omnibus Budget Reconciliation Act of 1990. US House of Representatives Conference Report to H.R. 5835. Washington, DC: US Government Printing Office; 1990. Report no. 101-P64.

42. US Dept of Health and Human Services. *State Medicaid Manual, Part 3-Eligibility HCFA-Pub 45-3.* Washington, DC: Health Care Financing Administration; March 1989.

43. US Dept of Health and Human Services. *Health United States 1991.* Hyattsville, MD: National Center for Health Statistics; 1992:5.

44. *An EBRI Special Report.* Washington, DC: The Employee Benefit Research Institute; February 1992:58.

45. *Securing Access to Health Care.* Washington, DC: President's Commission for the Study of Ethical Problems in Medicine and Biomedical and Behavioral Research: 1983:22. GPO 418–1801.

CHAPTER FOUR

Children in Search of a Home

Despite the affluence of the 1980s, there were more homeless Americans in that decade than at any other time since the Great Depression. The National Coalition for the Homeless places the number of homeless between 2 and 3 million. The US Department of Housing and Urban Development (HUD) issued a report in April 1984 in which Samuel R. Pierce, Jr, acknowledged the growing number of young women and children among the ranks of the homeless. "Today that population [the homeless] consists of more women, more minorities, more family members, more persons with mental illness, and more young persons than in the past."[1]

Because of the invisible dynamics of homeless families and children, it is difficult to provide a definitive calculation of their numbers. In an attempt to count the homeless population, the Bureau of the Census sent 15,000 interviewers to 22,000 shelters and open-air sites on the night of March 20, 1990. The Bureau of the Census concluded that

there were 230,000 homeless people.[2] This number, however, is inaccurate. The census excluded cities with populations under 50,000 and prohibited workers from counting the homeless who were not at designated sites. A later study commissioned by the Bureau of the Census revealed that the 1990 census failed to account for 70% of the homeless in Los Angeles and 47% in New York City.[3]

Although it is difficult to provide a definitive number of the homeless, it is generally agreed that families are the fastest growing segment of the homeless population. The Institute of Medicine released a report estimating that 100,000 of America's children fall asleep homeless every night.[4] The following numbers from the United States Conference of Mayors provide a general overview of families and urban homelessness in 1992.[5]

- Children comprise 20% of the homeless population.
- Requests for shelter by homeless families increased 72%.

- Families constitute 32% of the homeless population.
- Children account for 63% of homeless family members.
- Eighty-two percent of the homeless families are headed by a single parent.

The Human Factor

Given the federal and state policies pertaining to families with children, this population is becoming increasingly disenfranchised and alienated from the mainstream of society. The plight of the woman and infant in front of the Plaza described in the introduction is a reality facing a multitude of children each day. The onset of this chapter framed the magnitude of homeless children in empirical terms. The following anecdotes frame their plight in human terms.[6]

Karen left high school early. She also left her hopes behind. Karen seems tired and angry most of the time. Karen is a 26-year-old Black female with three small children who lives in Charleston, North Carolina. Karen is three months pregnant. Her three children are too young to attend school. Raymond is four and hyperactive. His mother struggles to contain his energetic outbursts in the shelter setting, afraid of losing her one safe place to stay. Angelica is two and a half. She has constant ear infections and chronic upper respiratory problems. Sleeping in a congregate setting is difficult for Angelica. Jamal is one year old. He has just learned to sit by himself. His developmental delays are becoming obvious to all. Housing is months away.

A 34-year-old female and a 35-year-old male with three young daughters and a son relocated to a Kansas City shelter from a vacant building. They were referred by Children's Mercy Hospital. Their Downs syndrome baby is on oxygen and has a visiting nurse six hours each day at the shelter. The goal planned with this family is family stabilization, employment for the father, and affordable housing. The mother's substance abuse problems have been a key factor in hindering more success at this point. The father has become employed full-time and they will soon move into Section 8 housing. Case management support will continue for one year.

Kim Johnson moved to Los Angeles from Colorado Springs. She brought her four-year-old son. They came looking for the husband/father who was already here. He is unemployed and homeless. They joined him in a homeless encampment. The child's encampment has become the playground. There are few, if any, amenities at the camp. The mother developed some health problems that she has been unable to care for. When found she was provided with temporary shelter, simply to allow her to recuperate her health. The child has had to act as an adult caring for her.

Mary, a mother of three children ages six, eight, and 12, is the head of a family that also includes a disabled sister. The five of them lived in a private market apartment complex in Chicago. She worked 40 hours a week. All the windows and doors of the first floor were broken or missing and drug dealers had moved in. They heard gunfire every night. Her children were propositioned and offered drugs in the elevator. One day, without notice as her children returned from school, she ordered them to pack their bags. They took the "ell" to the bus station and left without providing anyone a forwarding address. She quit her job with no notice. She arrived in St. Paul and went to a shelter and signed up for AFDC. She is willing to start all over —just to be safe. When asked why she came to St. Paul she answered: "Because I don't know anybody."

The Medical Impact

Several studies have shown that homeless children have extremely limited access to health care. Roth and Fox conducted a study on access to health care for homeless children living in a Philadelphia shelter. Their study found that 23.3% of the children did not have a regular source of health care, which is nearly twice the rate of low-income children living in the Philadelphia area.[7]

Miller and Lin studied homeless children living in shelters in King County, Washington, which includes Washington's largest city, Seattle. Overall, the percentage of homeless children reported to be in poor health was four times greater than the general pediatric population of the United States.[8] Almost half the children reported acute and chronic health care problems.[9]

Grants from the Robert Wood Johnson Foundation, Pew Memorial Trust, and the US Conference of Mayors established the Health Care for the Homeless Programs in 1984. The Health Care for the Homeless Programs implemented health care projects for the homeless in 19 cities. The Social and Demographic Institute of the University of Massachusetts conducted a study of the program in the mid-1980s. The study compared the health status of homeless children treated by the Health Care for the Homeless Programs with the health status of randomly sampled children who were part of the National Ambulatory Medical Care Survey.

The study measured 42 different conditions and disorders, from cancer to abrasions, and found that the health status of homeless children is unequivocally compromised.[10] The children of the National Ambulatory Medical Care Survey fared far better than those treated by the Health Care for the Homeless Programs. Table 4.1 compares the results of the National Ambulatory Medical Care

Table 4.1

Relative Frequency of Health Problems among Homeless and Other Children

Health Problem	Relative Frequency in Homeless Children
Seizure disorders	Sevenfold
Heart disease	Fourfold
Vascular disorders	Sixfold
Hypertension	Nearly twofold
Ear conditions	Nearly twofold
Gastrointestinal disorders	Nearly threefold
Dentition problems	Eighteenfold
Nutritional deficiencies	Nearly thirtyfold
Anemia	Nearly threefold
Minor upper respiratory infection	Nearly threefold
Serious upper respiratory infection	One-and-a-half times
Minor skin disorders	Fourfold
Serious skin disorders	Twofold
Lice	Thirty-fivefold
Infectious diseases	Nearly twofold
Abrasions	Nearly threefold

Source: S. Kyder-Coe. *Homeless Children and Youth*. New Brunswick, Transaction Publishers; 1991:84–85.

Survey and the Health Care for the Homeless Programs for children between infancy and 12 years of age. [11]

The Cognitive and Socioemotional Impacts

The cognitive status of homeless children is seriously compromised. A survey of homeless children living in Philadelphia shelters found that the cognitive and developmental status of homeless children lagged behind their housed peers as early as preschool. Homeless preschoolers, for example, were below age expectations in receptive vocabulary and visual motor skills.[12] The Philadelphia study also found that school-age children had low scores in expressive vocabulary and word decoding.[13]

Homeless children have high rates of absenteeism and failure in school. The failure rate for homeless children in Los Angeles is almost 30%.[14] A study of homeless school-age children in New York City shows that the majority of homeless children actually attending school have reading and mathematics skills that are far below their grade level.[15] A study conducted by Advocates for Children of New York, Inc., found that the holdover rate of homeless children in New York City seemed contingent on their length of homelessness.[16] Children that had been homeless for a year or more had a holdover rate of 17.8%, whereas children who had been homeless for less than 12 months had a holdover rate of 12.5%.[17]

Many studies have delved into the psychosocial development of homeless children. A study conducted by Bassuk and Rosenberg compared children from homeless families living in Boston shelters headed by a woman and poor children in female-headed households who resided in a home. The study employed the Denver Developmental Screening Test and the Simmons Behavior Checklist for children. The Denver Developmental Screening Test measures language, gross motor, fine motor, and social skills for children under the age of six. Table 4.2 shows the results of the Denver Developmental Screening Test employed by Bassuk and Rosenberg. Their study found that homeless children lagged significantly behind housed children, even though the latter group also lived below

Table 4.2
The Denver Developmental Screening Test:
A Comparison between Homeless Children and Housed Children

Test Result	Percentage of Homeless Children	Percentage of Children with Home
At least one lag	54	16
Type of lag		
Language	42	13
Gross motor	17	4
Fine motor	15	1
Personal/social	42	3

Source: Bassuk and Rosenberg. Psychosocial characteristics of homeless children and children with homes. *Pediatrics.* March 1990; 85:259.

the poverty threshold in a female-headed household.[18] Overall, 54% of the homeless children exhibited at least one major developmental delay, compared with 16% of the housed children.[19] Given the disparities in language, gross motor, fine motor, and social skills between the two groups, homeless children are at an extreme cognitive and socioemotional disadvantage early in their lives—a disadvantage that, in many instances, may be insurmountable.

Homelessness can have a devastating psychological effect on a child, which generally takes the form of anxiety, depression, and behavioral disturbances. Over a 2-week period, Kovacs administered the Children's Depression Inventory to 44 homeless children in Pittsburgh.[20] His study found that 54% of the children were in need of psychiatric intervention and 31% were clinically depressed.[21] Fox et al. conducted a study of homeless families housed in New York City hotels.[22] The children had severely compromised verbal functioning and psychomotor ability. The study also revealed that 38% of the children had emotional and behavioral problems.[23]

The Federal Response

The number of homeless families has exploded in recent years. A decrease in affordable housing, unemployment, reduced welfare benefits, and reduced federal housing assistance are major contributors to the homelessness crisis. The ranks of homeless families are growing and an enormous percentage of families

are living on the brink of homelessness. A typical poor family of four spends 70% of its income on housing, which leaves $3.49 a day for their other living expenses.[24] In 1989, in an effort to avoid homelessness, nearly 5 million children and their families doubled up with friends or relatives.[25]

Since 1980, the federal government has shifted its focus away from the construction, subsidization, and operation of public housing. In 1978, 32.1 billion federal dollars were appropriated for housing.[26] By 1988, however, only 9.8 billion federal dollars were appropriated for housing, which represents an 80% reduction in inflation-adjusted dollars.[27] On average, the federal government assisted 316,000 new households in fiscal years 1977 through 1980.[28] During the 1980s, however, HUD assisted an average of 76,000 new households, nearly a 76% decline from the 1970s.[29] Had HUD adhered to its commitments made during the late 1970s, an additional 2.4 million low-income households would be receiving federal assistance.[30]

The 1980 Depository Institutions and Monetary Control Deregulation Act and the Garn–St. Germain Act of 1982 that deregulated the savings and loan industry were instrumental in restricting the availability of low-income housing. The Depository Institutions and Monetary Control Deregulation Act allowed the banks to increase their consumer loan and credit card interests. The Garn–St. Germain Act authorized emergency assistance, increased investment, and augmented lending powers. Prior to 1980, the savings and loan industry was the primary financier for housing. After deregulation, however, the industry pursued other ventures that were far more speculative. The Tax Reform Act of 1986 also had a negative impact on the building of low-income housing because it terminated the tax status of industrial development bonds. Before the Tax Reform Act of 1986, state and local agencies used the bonds to offer financing for low-income families. Because the bonds were below the existing market rates, they enabled low-income families to purchase housing. As legislation whittled away financial sources for low-income housing, the HUD budget was slashed.

In 1987, the Stewart B. McKinney Act became law. The McKinney Act was to provide emergency relief to the homeless. Although the McKinney Act consolidated 20 different provisions for the homeless, it did not completely remedy the federal government's disjointed policy toward homelessness.[31] McKinney funds are distributed through competitive grants, block grants, and formula allocations.[32] The McKinney Act has been underfunded. Between 1987 and 1991, Congress authorized $3.4 billion for the McKinney Act but allocated only $2.3 billion.[33] In 1992, President Bush projected an appropriation of $776 million for the McKinney Act, even though Congress had authorized $1.13 billion.[34]

The Bush administration did little to ease the plight of homeless families. Only 36%, or 2.7 million, of the nation's 7.5 million poor households received a federal, state, or local rent subsidy.[35] Consequently, 4.8 million poor households, which invariably include millions of children, received no housing assistance during the late 1980s.[36] The median income of Section 8 recipients is $7,941 a year, and Section 8 waiting lists are measured more often by years rather than months. The program has been far from a panacea for America's homeless families.[37]

To combat homelessness, the Bush administration proposed two primary programs. The Home Ownership Opportunities for People Everywhere (HOPE)—which was the cornerstone of Bush's proposed housing policy—provides capital for public-housing tenants to purchase their dwellings. HOPE does not provide new low-income housing. The Home Investment Partnership Program (HOME) was to allocate $2 billion to states and municipalities for the building of affordable housing. Because HOME has targeted individuals with higher incomes than the vast majority receiving subsidized housing, the program draws funds from the other programs that serve a poorer population. It was discovered in 1993 that only 2% of the $2.5 billion set aside for the HOME program had actually been spent.[38]

References

1. *A Report to the Secretary on the Homeless and Emergency Shelters.* Washington, DC: US Dept of Housing and Urban Development, Office of Policy, Development and Research. 1984. No. 35-941.

2. Blau J. *The Invisible Poor.* New York: Oxford; 1992:26.

3. Ibid., 26.

4. *Homeless, Health and Human Needs.* Washington, DC: Institute of Medicine; 1988:13–14.

5. *A Status Report on Hunger and Homelessness in America's Cities: 1992.* Washington, DC: The United States Conference of Mayors. 1992:35.

6. Ibid., 44, 46.

7. Roth L, Fox E. Children of homeless families: Health status and access to care. *Journal of Community Health.* August 1990, 15:282.

8. Miller D, Lin E. Children in shelter homeless families: Reported health status and use of health services. *Pediatrics.* May 1988; 81:668.

9. Ibid.

10. Kyder-Coe S. *Homeless Children and Youth.* New Brunswick, NJ: Transaction Publishers; 1991:84–85.

11. Ibid.

12. Parker R. et al. A survey of homeless children in Philadelphia shelters. *American Journal of Diseases in Children.* May 1991; 145:520.

13. Kyder-Coe S. *Homeless Children and Youth.* New Brunswick, NJ: Transaction Publishers: 1991:84–85.

14. Wood D. Homeless children: Their evaluation and treatment. *Journal of Pediatric Health Care.* 1989:194–197.

15. Kyder-Coe S. *Homeless Children and Youth.* New Brunswick, NJ: Transaction Publishers; 1991:123–126.

16. Ibid.

17. Ibid.

18. Bassuk E, Rosenberg L. Psychosocial characteristics of homeless children and children with homes. *Pediatrics.* March 1990; 85:257-261.

19. Ibid.

20. Kyder-Coe S. *Homeless Children and Youth.* New Brunswick, NJ: Transaction Publishers; 1991:107.

21. Ibid.

22. Fox S. et al. Psychopathology and developmental delay in homeless children: A pilot study. *Journal of the Academy of Child and Adolescent Psychiatry.* September 1990; 29:732–734.

23. Ibid.

24. *An Opinion Maker's Guide to Children in the Election Year 1992: Leave No Child Behind.* Washington, DC: Children's Defense Fund; 1991:44.

25. Ibid.

26. Blau J. *The Visible Poor.* New York: Oxford University Press; 1992:71–72.

27. Ibid., 71–72.

28. Ibid., 71–72.

29. Leonard P, Lazere E. *A Place to Call Home.* Washington, DC: Center on Budget and Policy Priorities; 1992: xviii.

30. Ibid.

31. Blau J. *The Visible Poor.* New York: Oxford University Press; 1992:71–72, 113.

32. Ibid., 113.

33. Ibid.

34. Ibid.

35. Lazere E, Leonard P, Dolbeare C, Zigas B. The low-income housing crisis in 44 Major Metropolitan Areas. In: *A Place to Call Home*. Washington, DC: Center on Budget and Policy Priorities; 1992:58.

36. Sheft M. Crisis in housing for the poor. The Minneapolis and St. Paul report. In: *A Place to Call Home*. Washington, DC: Center on Budget and Policy Priorities; 1992:22.

37. Casey C. *Characteristics of HUD Assisted Renters and Their Units in 1989*. Washington, DC: US Dept of Housing and Urban Development, Office of Policy Development and Research; 1992:11.

38. $17.5 billion in HUD funds unused. *Minneapolis Star Tribune*. Wednesday, March 31, 1993:12A.

CHAPTER FIVE

Hunger in the Cities and in the Heartland

Although hunger is not as pervasive now as it was in the Great Depression, it has once again become a serious concern in the United States. Reductions in Aid to Families with Dependent Children (AFDC), unemployment insurance, and food-stamp assistance have significantly contributed to the escalation of hunger in both the urban and rural United States. Food shelves and soup kitchens are flourishing. Families with children are the fastest growing segment of the homeless, so it is not surprising that they are also the fastest growing users of emergency food assistance.

How can it be that in the United States—the greatest producer of agricultural products in the world—children are missing meals? In the 1960s, reports of hunger and malnutrition led to the creation and expansion of various supplemental nutritional programs such as the food-stamp program, the National School Feeding programs (breakfast and lunch), and the Special Supplemental Food Program for Women, Infants, and Children (WIC). In the early 1980s, children were still going hungry, lacking adequate nutrition from conception through infancy, early childhood, and into the school-age years.

A four-month-old infant in a state of shock was admitted to the emergency room of a Chicago hospital. She was dehydrated and lethargic and had suffered diarrhea over the course of the preceding four days. Her pulse was dangerously slow and her temperature was too low to measure. The infant was admitted to the intensive care unit after intubation and resuscitation in the emergency room. Her weight on admission was 6 pounds and 9 ounces, which was below the fifth percentile for her age and height. Her serum albumin was borderline and she had developed edema. The pediatricians on staff concluded that she had marasmus and kwashiorkor, which are conditions common to emaciated children during Third World famines.

A 2½-year-old child in Boston was dropped from the WIC program because her mother did not meet the program's necessary administrative requirements. Before the child's banishment from the WIC program, her weight was 28 pounds, which is normal for her age. Her weight, however, fell to 22 pounds within eight months. During this period the child suffered from third-degree malnutrition, and her weight at the age of three years and two months was that of a 14-month-old infant. After the child incurred severe pneumonia and anemia, she was reenrolled in the WIC program.

A 14-year-old girl visited a medical clinic in Grafton, West Virginia. She complained of debilitating abdominal pain. Her eyes were sunken and her belly was bloated. As her initial interview concluded, she revealed that she and her brothers and sisters would rummage through the dumpsters of local supermarkets in an effort to salvage their nightly dinner.[1]

US policymakers in the 1980s failed to heed the cries of hunger resonating from America's children. Although hunger has become more pronounced throughout the 1980s, former Attorney General Edwin Meese, III, declared the

following at a press conference.

I don't know of any authoritative figures that there are hungry children. I've heard a lot of anecdotal stuff, but I haven't heard any authoritative figures. . . . These allegations [of hunger] have been unsubstantiated until now. . . . Some of the allegations are purely political. . . . I don't believe that I have ever seen an authoritative study [on hunger]. . . . We've had considerable information that people go to soup kitchens because the food is free and that that's easier than paying for it.[2]

Despite this denial of hunger, the Physician Task Force on Hunger from Harvard University released evidence of the existence of hunger in a monumental report, "Hunger in America—A Growing Epidemic," in May 1985. The report estimated that the problem of hunger in the United States was much more widespread and serious than at any other time since the 1960s.[3] The Community Childhood Hunger Identification Project (CCHIP) surveyed families at or below 185% of the poverty threshold with at least one child under the age of 12. CCHIP found malnutrition and hunger in nearly 5.5 million children under the age of 12 in this country.[4] An additional 6 million children under 12 are at risk of hunger.[5] Consequently, one in four US children under the age of 12 suffers from hunger or is at risk of hunger.[6]

Hunger in the Cities

By the end of 1984, the Congressional Research Service of the US Congress documented 11 studies that were both national and local in scope, and addressed the problem of increasing hunger.[7] The first of these reports was published by the US Conference of Mayors in the fall of 1982. The report surveyed 55 cities and stated that 73% of the cities identified food as the "emergency service" most in demand.[8] In June 1984, the US Conference of Mayors released a followup report that provided an in-depth look at eight US cities: Cleveland, Denver, Detroit, Nashville, New Orleans, Oakland, Rochester (NY), and San Antonio. The report concluded that hunger is perhaps the "most prevalent and detrimental problem facing American cities today."[9] In 1992, the US Conference of Mayors disclosed the following.[10]

■ Demand for emergency food assistance for families with children increased in 82% of the surveyed cities.

■ Over two thirds of those requesting assistance were families with children.

■ An estimated 21% of requests went unmet last year because of a lack of resources.

■ Families requesting emergency food assistance increased by 50% in New York and Philadelphia and 43% in Los Angeles.

Hunger in the Heartland

The preceding section described the hunger that pervades our major cities. Hunger is also present outside metropolitan areas and urban centers, even though it is largely unnoticed. In Minnesota, for example, the center of the heartland, the use of emergency food shelves increased by over 300% during the 1980s.[11]

In January 1986, the Physician Task Force on Hunger in America, sponsored by the Harvard School of Public Health, released "Hunger Counties, 1986: The Distribution of America's High Risk Areas." The report showed that hunger was not concentrated exclusively in the cities, as many assumed, but rather in 150 counties in the agricultural heartland of the United States.[12]

Identification of the hunger counties was a tri-factorial process. First, counties with more than 20% of their population living below the federal poverty level were identified. Seven hundred sixteen, or roughly 23%, of the 3,142 US counties had 20% of their population living below the federal poverty level. Second, food-stamp eligibility for the county was calculated. Third, the actual number of people who received food-stamp assistance was determined. Given these criteria, the Physician Task Force on Hunger in America identified 150 hunger counties.[13]

There were no hunger counties in the northeastern states, West Coast states, Alaska, or Hawaii. The 150 hunger counties were dispersed in 24 states throughout the midwestern, southern, and western US census regions.[14] Although one might expect the majority of the hunger counties to be located among the "old poor" of Appalachia or possibly the "new poor" of the southwest, nearly half of the hunger counties (73) were located in 6 states of the Midwest, the nation's heartland:

- North Dakota (28)
- Missouri (17)
- South Dakota (11)
- Nebraska (10)
- Minnesota (5)
- Iowa (2)[15]

Despite the popular conception that hunger and malnourishment are an urban concern, 90% of the hunger counties were outside metropolitan areas. Hunger exists in the very regions that produce the majority of our nation's food.

The Task Force on Hunger in America found that 20 million Americans suffered from hunger in the mid-1980s. This original estimate was amended to 30 million in 1992.[16] There are an estimated 30 million Americans suffering from hunger—5.5 million of whom are children under the age of 12—and 90% of the hunger counties are in rural areas.

The Medical Impact

Hunger and malnutrition have a profound effect on the physical, cognitive, and socioemotional development of a child from conception to adolescence. The nutritional status of a pregnant mother plays an integral role in the health of her newborn. Low birthweight (5½ pounds or less) is one of the most crucial factors in the abnormal growth and development of an infant. The Institute of Medicine at the National Academy of Sciences has found that low birthweight is invariably linked to the poor nutritional status of a mother before and during pregnancy.[17] The Harvard Medical School and the National Institute of Mental Health have found that children born to malnourished mothers suffered from low birthweight, and proved to be more dependent on adults, less friendly, and much more withdrawn.[18]

The malnutrition described on page 45, resulting in marasmus and kwashiorkor, is produced by a severe deprivation of protein, calories, vitamins, and minerals. A child suffering from marasmus and kwashiorkor has edema and gross wasting, and is usually physically stunted. The mortality rate for these children is over 20% in Third World countries.[19]

The medical complications resulting from severe malnutrition are many and varied, ranging from anatomical deformation to renal malfunction. Although severe malnutrition exists in our nation, undernourishment—the deprivation of essential nutrients—is far more prevalent. Low-income elementary school children have inadequate intakes of vitamins and minerals.[20] Table 5.1 shows the conditions associated with vitamin deficiencies in infants and children.[21] The CCHIP studies found that many health problems were far more prevalent among children who suffered

Table 5.1

Vitamin Deficiencies and Accompanying Conditions

Nutrient	Population	Condition
Vitamin A	Preschoolers	Keratomalacia
Vitamin B1	Infants and preschoolers	"Wet" beriberi
Vitamin B6	Infants	B responsive seizures
Vitamin B12	Young infants Schoolchildren	Failure to thrive (FTT) Pernicious anemia
Biotin	Infants	Seborrheic dermatitis
Vitamin C	Infants Schoolchildren	Infantile scurvy Scurvy
Vitamin D	Schoolchildren	Rickets
Vitamin E	Preterm infants	Anemia, intracranial bleeding, retinopathy, lung disease
Folacin	Infants	Growth retardation
Vitamin K	Newborn infants	Hemorrhagic disease of the newborn

Source: Nestle Nutrition Workshop Series; 1990.

Table 5.2

Relative Frequency of Health Problems Experienced by Hungry Children Versus Low-income Children

Health Problem	Relative Frequency in Hungry Children
Unwanted weight loss	Threefold
Fatigue	Fourfold
Irritability	Threefold
Dizziness	Twelvefold
Headaches	Twofold
Ear infections	Twofold
Concentration problems	Threefold
Colds	Twofold

Source: Community Childhood Hunger Identification Project; 1991.

from hunger than low-income children who did not.[22] Table 5.2 shows the results of the CCHIP study. There is a strong correlation between infection and malnourishment. Infection is one of the preeminent factors in the morbidity and mortality associated with malnutrition.[23] Puffer and Serrano have shown that nutritional deficiencies played an integral role in 60.9% of the childhood deaths caused by infectious diseases.[24]

The Cognitive and Socioemotional Impacts

Although it is difficult to isolate and measure the effects of hunger and malnutrition on children, researchers are in consensus that hunger has a negative impact on the cognitive, social, and physical development of children. Because undernourished children are more anxious and less social and have limited concentration spans, their reading abilities, verbal skills, and motor skills suffer.[25]

Ernest Pollitt conducted research on hunger and learning. In a carefully controlled laboratory setting, Pollitt had well-nourished, middle-class children ranging from 9 to 11 years in age perform problem-solving tasks. Then he had the children perform the same tasks after they had been deprived of breakfast. Pollitt found that the absence of breakfast had an adverse effect on the speed and accuracy with which the children responded to the problem-solving tasks.[26] A similar study by Dr. Keith Conners yielded nearly identical results.[27]

Iron deficiency anemia is a form of malnutrition common among America's children. Studies have found that iron-deficient infants and children deomonstrate inferior performance on developmental and cognitive tests when compared with their peers with diets sufficient in iron. Even mild cases of iron deficiency anemia produce shortened attention span, irritability, fatigue, and diminished concentration abilities. Iron-deficient children do poorly in vocabulary, reading, mathematics, and psychological tests.[28]

Children's Hunger and the Federal Response

In the preceding sections of this chapter, we examined the prevalence of hunger among our children and its injurious and, at times, deadly consequences. Because the private sector cannot address a problem of this magnitude, the federal government must intervene; however, it cut 12.2 billion inflation-adjusted dollars from the food-stamp and child-nutrition programs from 1982 to 1985.[29] Although the cuts have been partially mitigated since then, they still have an indelible impact on our children.

The Food-Stamp Program

The food-stamp program provides a monthly supplement of food stamps to households whose gross monthly income falls below 130% of the federal poverty level.[30] Ninety-seven percent of food stamps are allocated to households with gross incomes at or below the poverty threshold.[31] At present, 50% of all food-stamp recipients are children, and 82% of households receiving food stamps include children.[32] The maximum food-stamp allotment for a family of four in 1991 was $352 a month, which translates to approximately 96 cents per meal, per person.[33] Only 18% of eligible households, however, are receiving the maximum allotment.[34]

Food stamps are a short-term remedy for households that have undergone an abrupt change hindering their ability to provide food for themselves. For example, 80% of the households enrolling in the food-stamp program have experienced the death of a head of household, departure of a gainfully employed adult, a young adult leaving the household, divorce, or a radical decline in income.[35] Seventy-five percent of food-stamp households leave the program after a remarriage, an increase in the number of adults in the household, a decrease in the household's size, or a $500 increase in income.[36]

The belief that food-stamp recipients waste their food stamps on junk food is popular myth. The facts, however, reveal the contrary. A US Department of Agriculture (USDA) study showed that food-stamp recipients, compared with shoppers from other economic strata, purchase between 7% and 29% more of the 11 nutrients studied per dollar spent.[37] Additional USDA studies have reported that food stamps increase the nutrients to qualifying households by 20% to 40%.[38]

CCHIP and other organizations have revealed that hunger during the 1980s had become nearly endemic for our nation's children. Eighty-two percent of the households receiving food stamps have children, and the food stamps have helped their recipients improve nutrition. It would make sense, then, that food stamps should be a national priority in the battle against childhood hunger. Despite the increasing hunger and malnutrition among our children and the deleterious consequences we have chronicled, the federal government has not responded to this crisis.

As the recession deepened in 1991, the ranks of those receiving food stamps increased by 10.8%.[39] This increased expenditure, however, was little more than a token gesture to the 30 million Americans suffering from hunger. According to a CCHIP survey, 37% of the families eligible for the food-stamp program were not receiving food stamps.[40] Sixty-five percent of those surveyed who were eligible for the food-stamp program but had never applied believed that their household did not meet the program's eligibility criteria.[41] Fifty-three percent of these families were hungry or at risk of hunger.[42]

The Special Supplemental Program for Women, Infants, and Children (WIC)

An amendment to the Child Nutrition Act of 1966 first established WIC in 1972. The WIC program provides supplemental food to low-income postpartum and nursing mothers and to infants and children up to age 5 who are diagnosed as nutritionally at risk. Food benefits are provided monthly through local health or community agencies. The supplements consist largely of dairy products, cereals, fruit and vegetable juices, and infant formula. Although the maximum income-eligibility standard is 185% of the federal poverty standard, states have the option of setting the threshold at 100% of the poverty threshold.

Numerous USDA studies and a 1992 Government Accounting Office (GAO) study have found the WIC program to be tremendously successful in terms of enhancing the nutritional status of mothers and their infants and also birth and infant outcomes. In 1986, the National WIC Evaluation was conducted for the USDA by the Research Triangle Institute and the New York State Research Foundation for Mental Health. The National WIC Evaluation, which consisted of four interrelated studies over the course of five years, found that the improved dietary intakes of protein, calories, and other nutrients in participating WIC mothers translated into the following beneficial outcomes for their newborns:

■ Increased length of gestation,
■ Decreased rate of preterm delivery,
■ Significant increases in birth-weight,
■ Reduced late fetal deaths, and
■ Increased infant head circumferences.[43]

Despite the significant benefits of the WIC program, it is a discretionary program, which means that it is limited by a federal ceiling. Consequently, WIC serves only 55% of those who are eligible.[44] According to a CCHIP survey, 31% of those who were eligible for the WIC program and not receiving WIC benefits were hungry or at risk of hunger.[45] Given that every dollar invested in the WIC program saves $3 in medical care, our government should not be so frugal when allocating monies for the WIC program.[46]

Child-Nutrition Programs

The child-nutrition programs include the National School Lunch Program, the School Breakfast Program, and the Summer Food Service Program for Children. They are administered by the USDA. The programs were designed to ensure that children from low-income families would receive at least one nutritious meal a day. Eligibility for the National School Lunch and Breakfast programs is based solely on income criteria. The USDA dictates that children from households below 185% of the poverty threshold are eligible for a partial deduction in the costs for their breakfast and lunch, while children living in households at or below 130% of the poverty threshold are eligible for a free breakfast and lunch. From 1982 to 1985, however, $12.2 billion were cut from the food-stamp and child-nutrition programs.[47] The cuts were made by lowering federal subsidies, altering income-eligibility criteria, and increasing the amount that families had to pay for a meal.

Despite increased expenditures since the 1980s, children's hunger is still on the rise, and participation in the National School Lunch Program has declined. In 1980, for example, 27 million children were participating in the National School Lunch Program; by

1990, however, that number had dwindled to 24.5 million.[48] The School Breakfast Program is suffering an even worse fate: Only 53% of the schools offering a lunch program are offering a breakfast program.[49] Consequently, only 30% of the children participating in the School Lunch Program receive school breakfast.[50] Only 41% of the households interviewed by CCHIP participated in the School Breakfast Program.[51]

The Summer Food Service Program for Children reached its peak in 1976, when 3.5 million children received summer meals.[52] Enrollment in the program plummeted to 1.4 million following the passage of the 1981 budgetary cuts. Although 12 million children received low-cost or free meals through the National School Lunch Program on a daily basis in 1991, only 1.8 million received summer meals.[53] A meager 22% of the households surveyed by CCHIP had children enrolled in the Summer Food Service Program.[54] Of the surveyed households who had never heard of the program or participated, 31% were hungry and 42% were at risk of hunger.[55]

WIC, food stamps, the National School Lunch Program, the School Breakfast Program, and the Summer Food Service Program for Children provide nutritional benefit to children, so it is unfortunate that in 1984 a national Task Force on Food Assistance recommended a plan to dismantle the federal anti-hunger effort developed over the past 15 years. That proposal would have eliminated or replaced such programs as food stamps, maternal and infant nutrition programs, and school meals with a state-run block grant model.[56]

References

1. *Health Consequences of Hunger on US Infants and Children.* Washington, DC: US Government Printing Office; 1985:26, 32, 91.

2. *Yes, Mr. Meese, There is Hunger in America.* Washington, DC: Center on Budget and Policy Priorities; December 1983.

3. Physician Task Force on Hunger in America, Harvard School of Public Health. *Hunger in America: The Growing Epidemic.* Middletown, Conn: Wesleyan University Press; 1985.

4. *Hunger in America, Its Effects on Children and Families, and Implications for the Future.* Washington, DC: US Government Printing Office; 1991:129.

5. Ibid.

6. Ibid.

7. *Summary of Reports Concerning Hunger in America, 1983–1984.* Washington, DC: Congressional Research Source; April 1984:3.

8. Ibid.

9. *Hunger in American Cities: Eight Case Studies.* Washington, DC: US Conference of Mayors; June 1983:3.

10. *A Status Report on Hunger and Homelessness: 1992.* Washington, DC: US Conference of Mayors; 1992.

11. Minnesota Food Education and Resource Center. *Homegrown Hunger—A Study of People Who Use Emergency Food Shelves in Minnesota.* Minneapolis: December 1985.

12. Physician Task Force on Hunger. *Hunger Counties 1986: The Distribution of America's High Risk Area.* Boston: Harvard School of Public Health; January 1986.

13. Ibid.

14. Ibid.

15. Ibid.

16. US hunger getting worse, with different profile. *American Medical News.* October 5, 1992.

17. *The Relationship Between Nutrition and Learning.* Washington, DC: National Education Association; 1989:12.

18. Ibid., 12.

19. Suskind RP, Bellinger M, Haas E, Lewinter-Suskind L. *Nestle Nutrition Workshop Series.* New York: Nestle Nutrition; 1990:4.

20. Morris, *Heading for a Health Crisis: Eating Patterns of America's School Children.* The Public Voice for Food. Washington, DC; 1991:4.

21. Suskind R, Lewinter-Suskind L. *Nestle Nutrition Workshop Series.* New York: Nestle Nutrition; 1990:19:122.

22. *Hunger in the United States.* Washington, DC: Campaign to End Childhood Hunger; 1992:3.

23. Suskind R, Lewinter-Suskind L. *Nestle Nutrition Workshop Series.* New York: Nestle Nutrition; 1990; 19:6.

24. Puffer R, Serrano C. The role of nutritional deficiency in mortality in childhood: Findings of the inter-American investigations of mortality in childhood. *Pan American Sanitary Bureau Bulletin;* 1973:7:29.

25. *The Relationship Between Nutrition and Learning.* Washington, DC: National Education Association; 1989:8.

26. Pollitt E. Developmental impact of nutrition on pregnancy, infancy, and childhood: Public health issues in the United States. *International Review of Research in Mental Retardation;* 1988: 51.

27. Conners K, Blouin A. Nutrition effects on the behavior of children. *J Psychiatr Res;* 1982:117:200–201.

28. Pollitt E. Developmental impact of nutrition on pregnancy, infancy, and childhood. In: Bray, NW, ed. *International Review of Research in Mental Retardation;* San Diego: Academic Press; 1988 15:52–57.

29. *Hunger in the United States.* Washington, DC: Campaign to End Childhood Hunger; 1992:2.

30. *Food Stamps: The Childhood Nutrition Program, Facts and Myths.* Washington, DC: Food Research and Action Center; 1991.

31. Ibid.

32. Ibid.

33. Ibid.

34. Ibid.

35. Ibid.

36. Ibid.

37. Ibid.

38. Ibid.

39. *A Survey of Childhood Hunger in the United States (Executive Summary).* Washington, DC: Community Childhood Hunger Identification Project; 1991.

40. Ibid.

41. Ibid.

42. Ibid.

43. *WIC Facts: National and State Profiles of the Special Supplemental Food Program for Women, Infants, and Children.* Washington, DC: Food Research and Action Center; 1988:4.

44. *Hunger in the United States.* Washington, DC: Campaign to End Childhood Hunger; 1992:7.

45. *A Survey of Childhood Hunger in the United States (Executive Summary)*. Washington, DC: Community Childhood Hunger Identification Project; 1991.

46. *Health Consequences of Hunger on US Infants and Children*. Washington, DC: US Government Printing Office; 1985:8.

47. *Hunger in the United States*. Washington, DC: Campaign to End Childhood Hunger; 1992:2.

48. *Annual Historical Review of FNS Programs*. Washington, DC: US Department of Agriculture; 1991:369.

49. *School Breakfast Score Card*. Washington, DC: Food Research and Action Center; 1992:12.

50. *Hunger in the United States*. Washington, DC: Campaign to End Childhood Hunger; 1992:7.

51. *A Survey of Childhood Hunger in the United States (Executive Summary)*. Washington, DC: Community Childhood Hunger Identification Project; 1991.

52. *Summer Food Service for Children*. Washington, DC: Campaign to End Childhood Hunger; 1992:1.

53. Ibid.

54. *A Survey of Childhood Hunger in the United States (Executive Summary)*. Washington, DC: Community Childhood Hunger Identification Project; 1991.

55. Ibid.

56. *Report of the President's Task Force on Food Assistance*. Washington, DC: US Government Printing Office; 1984:91.

CHAPTER SIX

The
Child Care
Puzzle

> "Clearly school children need supervision before and after school. What is not so clear is our nation's resolve to meet these children's needs."
>
> —ROGER NEUGEBAUER

The economic pressures posed by our society over the course of the past 20 years have irrevocably altered the dynamics of the nuclear family. The myth of the family consisting of a male breadwinner, female homemaker, and two children dissolved long ago. In 1990, 65% of school-age children had mothers in the out-of-home labor force.[1] Twenty-five percent of these children were reared in single-parent households, 90% of which are headed by women.[2]

The dissolution of the traditional American family has given rise to the child care industry. In 1990, 5.1 million preschool children were enrolled in child care facilities, and 2.5 million school-aged children under the age of 13 were enrolled in child care facilities.[3] Thus, a total of 7.6 million children under 13 years of age were enrolled in child care facilities in 1990.[4] However, 34 million children under the age of 13 were not enrolled in a child care facility on a regular basis.[5]

Parental Leave

High-quality child care is a puzzle with many pieces—pieces that include day care, nursery schools, preschool education, early intervention programs, family day care, and center-based programs. What are the relevant standards and costs of each of these pieces? If we are to provide a thorough examination of high-quality child care, we must explore its many facets.

Because 54% of the mothers in the out-of-home labor force have infants less than 1 year of age, it is appropriate to explore parental leave before examining the other pieces of the child care puzzle.[6] In 1990, President Bush vetoed a bill that would have provided unpaid parental leave after the birth of an infant or the adoption of a child. The business community and the US Chamber of Commerce were tenaciously opposed to the legislation. Although the maternity-leave bill signed by President Clinton seems like a victory for working mothers, it still

Table 6.1
Paid Maternal Leave in Selected Western Countries

Country	Duration of Leave	Percentage of Wage
Sweden	12 months	90
Finland	11 months	80
Denmark	24 weeks	90
Italy	5 months	80
Norway	18 weeks	100
Austria	16 weeks	100
France	16 weeks	90
Canada	15 weeks	60
Germany	14 weeks	100
Belgium	14 weeks	80
Ireland	14 weeks	80
Portugal	3 months	100
Israel	12 weeks	75
Greece	12 weeks	60
Netherlands	12 weeks	100
United States*	12 weeks	0

Source: Kamerman SB. Childcare policies and programs: An international overview. Journal of Social Issues. 1991:47, 179–196.
*Family and Medical Leave Act of 1993.

falls far short of the support offered by other Western countries. Because the bill includes mothers working only in businesses with more than 50 employees, it ultimately excludes millions of working mothers. Table 6.1 represents the maternal-leave policies of selected countries.[7]

The Negative Impacts of Forsaking Maternal Leave

From birth, a newborn seeks to bond with its mother by the reflex actions of contact-seeking, rooting, and sucking. This bonding is necessary for the infant's ability to form human relationships later in life.[8] The mother's capacity to nurture her infant is augmented by the infant's father. Recent evidence suggests that an infant's intellectual development is enhanced by a nurturing father.[9]

A growing number of professionals have realized that an infant's secure attachment to his or her parents through the first year of life is essential for normal development. A secure attachment has a tremendous impact on the development of self-esteem, competence, problem-solving ability, and achievement during the school years. The "strange situation," an attachment paradigm developed by psychologist Mary Ainsworth, has produced numerous followup studies. The "strange situation" involves a mother leaving her baby in the company of a stranger. The "securely attached" babies who have had consistent, responsive mothering are upset when their mothers leave the room. When the mother returns, the "securely attached" babies crawl to their mothers, longing for comfort and attention. The "anxious resistant" and "anxious avoidant" babies have different reactions. The "anxious resistant" babies, as a rule, have had unpredictable mothering, and display anger and ambivalence when reunited with their mothers. The "anxious avoidant" babies generally do not cry when their mothers leave the room and avoid their mothers when they return to the room.

Studies employing the "strange situation" experiment have found that infants who are placed in day-care settings were more likely to avoid their mothers than home-reared infants.[10] Longitudinal studies have shown that 3-year-olds and 4-year-olds placed in day care during early infancy had a tendency to be much more physically and verbally abusive than children raised at home throughout their infancy.[11] A study of kindergartners and first graders by the University of North Carolina demonstrated that children who were reared in day care as young infants were much more physically and verbally abusive than their home-reared counterparts.[12] These and similar results on studies pertaining to day care versus home care in early infancy demonstrate why the majority of Western countries place such importance on paid maternal leave.

Child Care for Preschool Children

The establishment of the Nursery for Children of Poor Women in New York in 1854 marks the beginning of day care in the United States. The Nursery for Children of Poor Women and other day-care centers were modeled after the French crèche, which was first established in Paris in 1844.[13] The majority of these early day-care centers were sponsored by churches, settlement houses, or voluntary social agencies. Their goal was to prevent child neglect during a mother's working hours and to examine whether the children of destitute parents were in need of institutionalization.

The US day-care or child care industry has been grossly inadequate in terms of affordability and quality, yet an increasing number of families are forced to rely on it. Four primary arrangements make up the vast majority of supplemental child care in the United States: center care, family day care, relative care, and in-home care.

- Center care is where children are cared for in a group and nonresidential setting for all or part of the day. Center-care facilities are for profit and nonprofit, and are sponsored by public schools, religious organizations, community agencies, various private organizations, etc. Center care provides child care to 18% of working mothers who have children three years of age and younger, and to 34% of working mothers who have children that are three to four years of age.

- Family day care is provided in the caregiver's home for a small number of children. Family day care is both regulated and unregulated, and is often provided by a mother who has children herself. Family care provides child care to 19% of working mothers who have children that are three years of age or younger, and to 13% of working mothers who have children between three and four.

- Relative care is given by a relative in the child's or relative's home. Relative care provides child care to 15% of working mothers who

have children three years of age or younger, and to 11% of working mothers who have children between three and four years of age.

- In-home care is supplied by a non-relative who comes to the family's home. In-home care provides child care to 2% of working mothers who have children three years and younger, and to 2% of working mothers who have children between three and four years of age.[14]

Preschool Child Care and Quality

According to the National Child Care Survey of 1990, 60% of the parents who used child care centers and family day-care centers felt that quality was the most important factor in their choice of facility.[15] High-quality child care, however, is an ambiguous concept. The federal government has balked at creating and implementing minimum standards of quality for the child care industry, even though the regulatory efforts of some states have been extremely lax.[16]

Despite the fact that the federal government has not issued a definitive set of recommendations for the child care industry, there are many studies that can provide legislators with a blueprint for quality-control legislation. These studies have found that toddlers who had been enrolled in high-quality care demonstrated higher adjustment ratings when placed in kindergarten.[17] Children placed in high-quality child care also have a higher degree of social competence and are more empathetic to their peers.[18]

The National Child Care Staffing Study examined the quality of care in 227 child care centers in five major cities.[19] The study found a direct connection between low-quality child care and high turnover rates of child care providers, which were ultimately linked to the low salaries of the child care workers.[20] The average hourly wage for day-care-center workers is $5.40, and the annual turnover rate is 41%.[21] The National Child Care Staffing Study found that 70% of US childcare centers provided less than quality care because of the low salaries paid to child care workers.[22]

Staff qualifications also play an integral role in high-quality child care. Children score better on tests of cognitive and social competence when their caregivers have more formal education and child-related training.[23] Caregivers who have had extended education and training have a tendency to be less authoritarian and punitive.[24] Despite the importance of staff qualifications, 35 states required no training for staff in family day care in 1990.[25]

The ratio of adults to children is an extremely crucial factor in high-quality child care. A study conducted by Howes found that the adult-to-child ratio is the preeminent factor in the determination of high-quality child care.[26] Children in smaller groups with high adult-to-child ratios are more verbal, less aggressive, and make greater progress in standardized tests that measure learning and vocabulary.[27] As the ratio of children to adults increases, the children are likely to experience fewer developmentally appropriate activities.[28] Despite these data, however, 19 states allow child care centers to operate with five or more infants per

Table 6.2—Suggested Child/Adult Ratios for Selected Age Groups		
Age of Child	Group Size	Ratios
Birth to 12 months	8	4:1
12 to 24 months	12	4:1
24 to 30 months	12	6:1
30 to 36 months	14	7:1
36 months	20	10:1
48 months	20	10:1

Source: National Association for the Education of Young Children.

adult, and Idaho allows a 1:12 adult-to-infant ratio.[29] Table 6.2 depicts the recommendations of the National Association for the Education of Young Children for appropriate child-to-adult ratios and maximum group sizes.

Home Alone

Given today's economic realities, an increasing number of households have both spouses working to make ends meet. In most cases, the additional worker does not provide extra "spending money" but rather the household's ability to meet the mortgage, utilities, health care, and child care expenses. As the percentage of women in the work force has escalated and the number of single-parent families has increased, children have been left alone and unsupervised before school, after school, and at night. Because many of these children wear a characteristic house key on a chain around their necks, they have become known as "latchkey kids."

The Children's Defense Fund estimates that there are more than 7 million latchkey kids.[30] The general consensus is that latchkey kids are between 5 and 13 years of age. Children younger than 5 are generally cared for in some way. Adolescents older than 14, on the other hand, are often considered old enough to care for themselves before and after school. (With the present atmosphere of illicit drugs, violence, teenage sexuality, depression, and teen suicide, however, we have strong reservations about this assumption. Although we do not feel that all adolescents need constant supervision, we question the arbitrary assumption that all 14-year-olds can safely remain unsupervised.)

The latchkey phenomenon has lingered in the public consciousness for over a decade, but the majority of state bureaucracies have scant information about school-age child care programs in their states. A School-Age Childcare (SACC) project conducted in 1990 found that only the child care licensing agencies of Ohio, New Hampshire, Vermont, and South Dakota were able to report the number of licensed, center-based, school-age child care programs in their respective states.[31] The SACC project also revealed major discrepancies in standards among the states' school-age child care standards. For example, in Maine, Montana, and New York, the state-mandated adult-to-child ratio was 1:10; in Texas, on the other hand, the mandated adult-to-child ratio was 1:26.[32]

The Medical Impacts of Latchkey Arrangements

The latchkey arrangement has a negative impact on children's physical health. A 1989 study of 4932 eighth-grade students found that the students who were left in self-care for more than 10 hours a week were nearly twice as likely to smoke cigarettes, drink alcohol, and use marijuana.[33] Abusive treatment by an older sibling is another danger for latchkey children. A survey conducted by Straus et al. found that severe physical assault was three times as likely to be carried out by older siblings as parents.[34] A study by Finkelhor reported that 39% of the sexual abuse of boys and 21% of the sexual abuse of girls was instigated by siblings.[35]

Unsupervised children are much more likely to be the victims of accidents—fires, falls, ingestion of toxic substances, etc.—which are the primary causes of death for children between the ages of 1 and 14.[36] Children can lose their lives or become severely impaired because of an accident that happens in a fraction of a second; yet millions of children are left alone daily. If children are properly supervised, how many of these accidents can be prevented?

The Cognitive and Socioemotional Impacts of Latchkey Arrangements

Researchers have found that the latchkey phenomenon has negative cognitive and socioemotional effects on school-age children. A survey conducted by Louis Harris and Associates asked both teachers and parents to rank seven possible causes of students' difficulties in school. The majority of the teachers chose "children left on their own after school" as a child's primary difficulty.[37] Sixty-two percent of teachers surveyed felt that children were left alone far too much after school.[38] Forty-one percent of the parents surveyed admitted to leaving their children on their own from the end of the school day to 5:30 P.M. at least once a week, and almost 25% left their children alone on a daily basis.[39]

The fear of being alone is the most common emotional complaint among self-care children. In 1984, *Sprint* magazine asked 7000 fourth-, fifth-, and sixth-graders to write about situations they found frightening. Nearly 70% of the respondents reported fear of being alone when their parents were working.[40] A study conducted by Long and Long interviewed 85 Black parochial-school children who were between the first and sixth grades in Washington, D.C. The latchkey children demonstrated elevated levels of fear compared with the children who were given continuous adult supervision. A study conducted in Minneapolis also found latchkey children far more fearful than their adult-supervised counterparts.[41] Studies show that the fears of latchkey children manifest themselves in many ways, ranging from nightmares to the frequent calling of their parents.[42]

The latchkey arrangement can take a social toll on the lives of children. In their Washington, D.C., study, the Longs reported that 80% of the latchkey children were not allowed to have visitors.[43] Because 40% of the children were not permitted to play outdoors or socialize, they were ultimately isolated.[44] A 1982 Department of Health and Human Services study of families in Virginia and Minnesota substantiated the isolation felt by latchkey children.[45]

Child Care and the Federal Response

Europeans pay for between 5% and 15% of their children's out-of-home child care; US parents, on the other hand, pay for well over 90% of their children's out-of-home child care.[46] Our government's lack of child care intervention throughout the 1980s and early 1990s has been partially responsible for this gap. Because high-quality child care is so costly, it is nearly impossible for low-income families to afford. In 1990, for example, the families of employed mothers who had children under 5 years of age spent up to 23% of their gross income on child care.[47]

Child care in the United States took a major step backward in the 1980s. The Family Support Act, the Social Services Block Grant, and Dependent Care Tax Credit have had little effect on the child care crisis.

In 1988, Congress passed the Family Support Act (FSA), which mandated that Aid to Families with Dependent Children (AFDC) families participating in job training and/or education programs be provided with child care. The federal government provided the FSA program with approximately $340 million in fiscal year 1992. Because federal grants for the program are contingent on the individual state matching funds, there are tremendous discrepancies in state funding for the program. The following trends have emerged.[48]

- Twenty-eight states receive FSA appropriations that either are exempt from basic health and safety regulations or meet the most rudimentary standards.
- Sixteen states served only 5% of the eligible population in 1990.
- Some states allocate so little for matching federal grants that they are unable to provide quality child care or provide adequate choices.

The Social Services Block Grant distributed $2.8 billion to the states in fiscal year 1992. The Social Services Block Grant does not mandate, however, that the states spend a certain percentage of the grant on child care, as was the case under Title XX of the Social Security Amendments of 1972. Title XX mandated that the states allocate a certain percentage of federal aid for child care, but Title XX lost its statutory impetus once it was absorbed by the Social Services Block Grant.

The Dependent Care Tax Credit enables families to claim a tax credit for a share of child care expenditures. Because the credit is determined on a sliding scale, lower income families have a higher credit. Because the credit is not refundable, families whose income is too meager to pay federal income tax do not benefit from the tax credit. A study has revealed that only 22% of mothers in the work force whose income is under $15,000 took advantage of the Dependent Care Tax Credit, while 37% of mothers in the work force earning over $50,000 a year claimed the tax credit.[49]

After an arduous legislative battle in 1990, the 101st Congress enacted the Child Care and Development Block Grant and the At-Risk Childcare Programs. The Child Care and Development Block Grant allocates $2.5 billion for low-income child care over 3 years. Dissemination of the funds is contingent on the individual state's per capita income, the number of children under 5 years old, and the number of children receiving free or partially subsidized lunch in the National School Lunch Program. Three-quarters of the block money must be allocated to expand the availability of child care. The remaining 25% of the grant monies is to be reserved for quality improvements in child care, early education, and latchkey programs. Parents with children under the age of 13 and incomes less than 75% of the state's median income are eligible for the program. The state must provide eligible parents with vouchers that enable them to pay for the registered, licensed, and regulated child care facility of their choice.

The At-Risk Child Care Program is intended to provide child care to low-income families who are close to applying for AFDC benefits. The states must provide matching funds, however, to qualify for the program. The federal government allocated $300 million in fiscal year 1992 for the At-Risk Child Care Program.

Because 34 million children under 13 years of age are without a regular source of child care, the federal child care legislation of 1990 is inadequate.[50] Seventy-five percent of the funds generated by the Child Care and Development Block Grant and the At-Risk child care Programs are funneled to low-income families, so the legislation will have only a minor impact on the child care problems of other families.[51] The impact of the legislation on low-income families in need of child care is debatable as well. California, for example, could subsidize child care for 25% of its eligible low-income families before passage of the Child Care and Development Block Grant and the At-Risk Child Care Program; after passage of the legislation, it can subsidize the child care of 30% of such families.[52]

References

1. Zigler E, Gillman E. Day care in America: What is needed? *Pediatrics.* January 1993 1:175.
2. Ibid.
3. *The Demand and Supply of Child Care in 1990.* Washington, DC: National Association for the Education of Young Children; 1991:16.
4. Ibid.
5. Ibid.
6. Zigler E, Gillman E. Day care in America: What is needed? *Pediatrics.* January 1993; 1:175.
7. Kamerman SB. Child Care policies and programs: An international overview. *Journal of Social of Issues.* 1991; 47:188.
8. Rinsley D. A child psychiatrist looks at child care. In: Schlafly P, ed. *Who Will Rock the Cradle.* Washington, DC: World Publishing. 1989:44-45.
9. Ibid.
10. Ibid., 61–62.
11. Ibid., 62.

12. Ibid.

13. Sidel R. *Women and Children Last—The Plight of Poor Women in Affluent America.* New York: Penguin; 1987:118.

14. *The Demand and Supply of Child Care in 1990.* Washington, DC: National Association for the Education of Young Children; 1991:15.

15. Ibid., 22.

16. Zigler E, Gillman E. Day care in America: What is needed? *Pediatrics.* January 1993: 1:175.

17. Howes C. Can the age of entry into childcare and the quality of child care predict adjustment in kindergarten? *Developmental Psychology.* 1990; 26:292–303.

18. Vandell D, Henderson V, Wilson K. A longitudinal study of children with day-care experiences of varying quality. *Child Development.* 1988; 59:1286–1292.

19. Schroeder P, Reder N. Ensuring quality, affordable child care: Mobilizing for action. *Pediatrics.* January 1993; 1:245.

20. Ibid.

21. Zigler E, Gillman E. Day care in America: What is needed? *Pediatrics.* January 1993; 1:175.

22. Ibid.

23. Clarke-Stewart A, Bruber C. Daycare form and features. In: Ainslie RC, ed. *Quality Variations in Daycare.* New York: Praeger; 1984.

24. Arnett J. Caregivers in day care centers: Does training matter? *Journal of Applied Developmental Psychology.* 1989; 10:541–552.

25. *Child Care: Key Facts.* Washington, DC: Children's Defense Fund; 1992:5.

26. Howes C. Caregiver behavior in center and family day care. *Journal of Applied Developmental Psychology.* 1983; 4:96–107.

27. Ruopp R et al. *Children at the Center: Final Report of the National Day Care Study.* Cambridge, Mass: Abt Associates; 1979.

28. Howes C, Phillips D, Whitebook M. Thresholds of quality: Implications for the social development of children in center based child care. *Child Development.* 1992; 63:449–460.

29. *Child Care: Key Facts.* Washington, DC: Children's Defense Fund; 1992:5.

30. Seligson M, Allenson M. Continuity of supervised care for school-age children. *Pediatrics.* 1993; 91:206.

31. Seligson M, Gannett E, Cotlin L. Before- and after-school child care for elementary school children. In: Spodek B, Saracho O, eds. *Yearbook in Early Childhood Education.* New York: Teachers College Press; 1992; vol. 3.

32. Ibid.

33. Ibid., 11.

34. Straus M, Gelles R, Steinmetz S. *Behind Closed Doors: Violence in the American Family.* New York: Doubleday-Anchor; 1980:83.

35. Finkelhor D. *Sexually Victimized Children.* New York: Free Press; 1979:89.

36. Miller B, Marx F. *After School Arrangements in Middle Childhood: A Review of the Literature.* Wellesley, Mass: School-Age Child Care Project; 1990:8.

37. Officials say latchkey programs not reaching low-income students. *Minneapolis Star Tribune.* September 3, 1987:10A.

38. Ibid.

39. Ibid.

40. Miller B, Marx F. *After School Arrangements in Middle Childhood: A Review of the Literature.* Wellesley, Mass: School-Age Child Care Project; 1990:8.

41. Ibid., 9.

42. Ibid., 8.

43. Ibid.

44. Ibid.

45. Ibid.

46. Scarr S et al. Quality of child care as an aspect of family and childcare policy in the United States. *Pediatrics.* January 1993; 1:182.

47. *The Demand and Supply of Child Care in 1990.* Washington, DC: National Association for the Education of Young Children; 1991:32.

48. *The State of America's Children 1992.* Washington, DC: Children's Defense Fund; 1992:20.

49. Ibid., 13.

50. *The Demand and Supply of Child Care in 1990.* Washington, DC: National Association for the Education of Young Children; 1992:16.

51. Zigler E, Gillman E. Day care in America: What is needed? *Pediatrics.* January 1993; 1:176.

52. Ibid.

Head
Start
Revisited

Although early education and child care may share parallel ambitions, their origins and objectives are markedly different. Child care in the United States was born of necessity for the working poor of New York City, whereas early education had its origins in the study and advancement of child psychology and child development. The first nursery school with an emphasis on child development was created in 1915 by a group of wives whose husbands were on the faculty at the University of Chicago.

Since 1915, numerous public and private early education programs have been implemented in the United States. The most notable of these programs is Head Start, which began in the 1960s. Head Start was a social experiment that instituted a marriage between low-income children, who were known to be at risk of school failure, and high-quality early education. In addition to addressing day care, the program authorized the creation of Head Start agencies, which were designed to provide comprehensive health, educational, nutritional, and social services to economically disadvantaged children between 3 and 5 years of age. Its ultimate objective was to endow the underprivileged children of our country with an experience that would enhance their lives. By the end of 1965, Head Start had 11,068 centers and enrolled 561,359 low-income preschoolers.[1] Head Start serves a diverse population in its effort to reach low-income children. Figures 7.1 and 7.2 offer an overview of the program's ethnic and age distribution.[2]

Head Start recently received an increase of funds and participation. Head Start served 621,078 children at a cost of $2.2 billion in 1992.[3] An additional allocation of $500 million enabled the program to serve 721,268 children in 1993.[4] Although the number of children enrolled in Head Start increased by over 100,000 from 1992 to 1993, only a third of the eligible children 3 to 5 years of age were

Figure 7.1—The ethnic composition of children in Head Start.

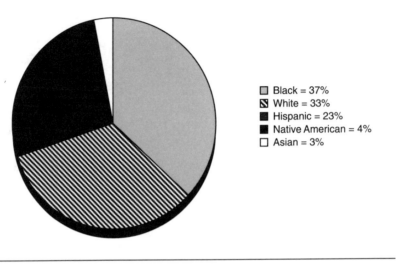

- ☐ Black = 37%
- ▧ White = 33%
- ■ Hispanic = 23%
- ■ Native American = 4%
- ☐ Asian = 3%

Source: Project Head Start Statistical Fact Sheet, January 1992.

Figure 7.2—The age distribution of children in Head Start.

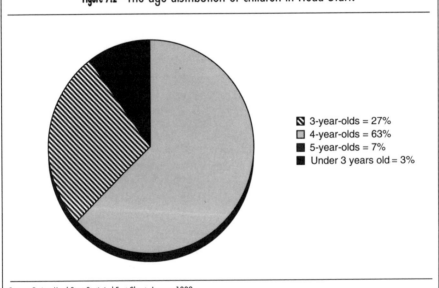

- ▧ 3-year-olds = 27%
- ☐ 4-year-olds = 63%
- ■ 5-year-olds = 7%
- ■ Under 3 years old = 3%

Source: Project Head Start Statistical Fact Sheet, January 1992.

actually enrolled in the program. The Clinton Administration, however, has promised full Head Start enrollment by 1999.

Given Head Start's legislative and fiscal impetus, it is the predominant form of early education in the United States for low-income children. Although this chapter will primarily focus on the Head Start program, it will also address other early education programs. Because many of these other programs have had better short-term and longitudinal outcomes than Head Start, the inclusion of their methodologies would greatly enhance the efficacy of the Head Start program. In addition, the positive outcomes achieved by some of these programs firmly establish the importance and necessity of early education.

The Four Components of Head Start

The Head Start program has four major components that should cater to all disadvantaged preschoolers between 3 and 5 years of age: education, health-care ministration, parental involvement, and social services intervention.[5]

The educational component of Head Start ensures that every child enrolled in the program receives a broad range of learning experiences that nurture intellectual, social, and emotional growth. Head Start's educational agenda is designed to meet a child's specific developmental, ethnic, and cultural needs.

The health component of Head Start has three primary dimensions. First,

every child enrolled in the program must receive a complete physical, which includes dental, hearing, and vision examinations and immunizations. If a specific malady or condition is identified, a followup is provided. Second, children enrolled in Head Start are served at least one hot meal and a snack per day. Head Start programs have a trained nutritionist who understands the dietary needs of children. The nutritionist also educates parents on the preparation of well-balanced meals and the procurement of food stamps, WIC vouchers, or other nutritional assistance. Third, every Head Start agency is required to have a mental-health professional available to assist parents and staff in understanding child growth and development in order to reach the overall goal of social competence.

Parents have the greatest impact on children, so Head Start attempts to include parents on many different levels. Head Start parents are involved in parent education classes, program planning, and various operational activities. Workshops and classes on child development and staff visits offer Head Start parents a greater understanding of the unique needs of their children and of home-based educational activities.

The social-service component of Head Start provides an assessment of a family's particular needs and matches the family with the services that attempt to address those needs. Information on community resources and programs, community outreach, crisis intervention, and emergency assistance are some of the ways the program helps families of Head Start children.

A Qualitative Look at Head Start

Head Start has come under fire because the cognitive progress made by its alumni diminishes as the children proceed through elementary school. As in child care, expenditures on staff and facilities are major variables in the determination of high-quality early education. Because the average expenditure per Head Start child decreased by 13% in inflation-adjusted dollars between 1981 and 1989, the qualitative dimension of the program suffered through the 1980s.[6] Because spending on the Perry Preschool project, a successful early education program, was two to three times greater than that of Head Start, it should not be surprising that children enrolled in the former register far better cognitive and developmental outcomes than Head Start children.[7]

A result of the Head Start cutbacks during the 1980s is a deterioration in the wages of Head Start teachers. In 1990, for example, Head Start teachers earned approximately $12,000 per year, which was 61% of the wage received by teachers in public schools.[8] The low wages of Head Start teachers translate into an annual turnover rate of roughly 25%.[9] High staff turnover in early education programs has a detrimental effect on children. In a 1989 study, Whitebrook et al. found a negative correlation between high staff turnover and the social and verbal development of children.[10]

The longevity of an early education experience plays a crucial role in its cognitive and developmental impact on a child. At present, 4-year-olds make up 63% of the children enrolled in Head Start.[11] Five-year-olds constitute only 7% of the program, even though 30% of low-income 5-year-olds are not enrolled in kindergarten.[12] Because the majority of children in Head Start are enrolled for only a year, they have shown lower cognitive outcomes than children in other early education programs with a longer enrollment term. Richards and Sielger have found that children tend to regress to previous levels if their special supports are withdrawn and they are placed in environments that do not foster the newly acquired cognitive gains.[13] For example, the Perry Preschool and the Institute for Developmental Studies early education programs—which lasted 2 and 5 years, respectively—have generally recorded far better cognitive and developmental outcomes than Head Start.[14,15]

Research and evaluation are another important aspect of early education. The funds allocated for research, demonstration projects, and evaluation for Head Start have declined considerably, however, during the past 15 years. In 1974, 2.5% of the Head Start budget was directed to research, evaluation, and experimentation.[16] During 1989, however, only 0.11% of the Head Start budget covered research, evaluation, and experimentation.[17] If Head Start is to sustain its gains and launch innovative new programs, larger allocations for research, demonstration projects, and evaluation are required.

The physical conditions of many Head Start facilities are run down, which invariably detracts from a high-quality education. The National Head Start Association conducted a survey of Head Start programs throughout the continental United States, Puerto Rico, American Samoa, and Guam. A third of the Head Start programs responding to the survey declared that their facilities were substandard, requiring repairs or replacement.[18] The projected cost of these renovations is between $93 and $178 million.[19]

Another problem for Head Start is its need for additional space. Few Head Start programs own their facilities. The average rent for an individual Head Start program is $70,000, or 6.8% of the program's budget.[20] Twenty-nine percent of Head Start facilities are in public schools.[21] Because of expanding preschool and kindergarten programs, many Head Start programs have had to relinquish space that had been donated. Obtaining adequate and affordable space is becoming an increasing problem for Head Start. If the program is to meet its future projections, it must be able to purchase or lease suitable facilities.

The Medical Impact of Early Education

As previous chapters have shown, health care and nutrition are necessary in the development of a child. Consequently, it is essential that a high-quality early education program accommodate children's health and nutrition needs. Although

Head Start has been attacked for the low cognitive scores of its participants, many of the program's critics have forgotten that it has provided millions of children with medical, dental, mental-health, and nutritional services. In fact, researchers have found that the Head Start snacks and meals provide 50% of the recommended nutrients required by a child.[22] Nearly all the children enrolled in Head Start for 90 days or more receive medical screening, and 97% of children needing medical services are given the required care.[23] Approximately 63% of Head Start children are channeled into Medicaid's Early Periodic Screening Diagnosis and Treatment (EPSDT) program, which covers their medical and dental care.[24]

There is a scarcity of data about Head Start children and their medical outcomes, and only a few studies have been conducted on the subject. Abt Associates, Inc., tested a group of Head Start children and children who were not affiliated with Head Start for different pediatric problems. The study found that the health status of Head Start children was considerably improved compared with that of the control group. Head Start children's pediatric problems were medically addressed by a 66% versus 43% margin.[25]

An early study of Head Start and health care outcomes was undertaken by Robert Ross in Seattle, Wash. The study compared the health status of 108 Head Start graduates, their older siblings, and a sample of middle-class children. Teachers graded the three groups of children on a number of criteria, ranging from physical health to motor development. Because there was no significant difference between the Head Start children and the middle-class children, Ross concluded that Head Start enables low-income children to achieve the same physical health as more advantaged children.[26]

Another study, conducted by Hale et al., examined the health screenings of 40 Head Start children, 18 children on a Head Start waiting list, and 20 children enrolled in a middle-class nursery school. The eight screenings were lead, hematocrit, tuberculosis, growth assessment, blood pressure, hearing, urine, and vision. Table 7.1 shows the health care screening disparities between the Head Start children and the children on the waiting list.[27]

Although Head Start participants lag behind those in other early education programs in cognitive outcomes, the Head Start program provides health care, nutritional, and other social services to low-income children. The program also improves socioemotional behavior and strengthens familial bonds.[28]

The Cognitive and Socioemotional Impacts

Many studies have measured the cognitive effect of early education on children. The majority of both short-term and longitudinal studies have noted positive results. Irving Lazar organized a consortium of 11 early education projects— only 2 of which were Head Start programs—that had been implemented between 1962 and 1972. The consortium administered a standardized questionnaire to the original children in the various programs: 3593 children originally participated in the 11 programs, and 2008—or 56%—were ultimately located. The first consortium study was in 1976, when the children being tracked were between 9 and 19 years of age. A second study occurred in 1979, when the children were between 12 and 22 years of age.

Table 7.1
A Comparison of Selective Health Screenings for Head Start Enrolled and Other Children

	Lead	Hematocrit	Tuberculosis	Growth Assessment	Blood Pressure	Urine	Vision	Hearing
Head Start	32	100	98	100	100	55	98	100
Waiting list	6	78	44	100	39	56	6	11
Middle class	20	95	80	100	69	75	20	30

Source: Hale B, Seitz V, Zigler E. Health services and Head Start: A forgotten formula. *Journal of Applied Developmental Psychology.* 1990;11.

Four of the consortium projects that had data 10 years or more beyond the children's early education experience found that school performance was significantly enhanced by a high-quality early education. Only 13% of the program children had been placed in special education classes by the end of high school, compared with 31% of the control group.[29] When all 11 projects of the consortium were averaged, it was found that 32% of the program children had repeated a grade, and 47% of the control group had repeated a grade.[30] Because the children in many consortium projects are still teenagers, it is not possible to give a definitive percentage of high school graduation outcomes; however, 65% of the children from four of the early education programs graduated from high school, compared with 52% of the children from the control groups.[31]

The Institute for Developmental Studies (IDS) early enrichment program uncovered a correlation between the IDS program and cognitive development. IDS tracked 1200 children from the mid-1960s through 1984. IDS children registered immediate enhancement of linguistic abilities and academic and self-esteem concepts.[32] Fifty-seven percent of IDS children graduated from high school; only 36% of the control-group children graduated from high school.[33]

The Perry Preschool project, a consortium study, identified a population of 3- and 4-year-olds who were living in poverty and randomly placed the children into two groups.[34] The first group received a high-quality early education; the latter group was excluded from an early education experience.[35] At age 7, the children in the Perry Preschool group recorded IQs that were, on average, 5 points higher than those of the control group.[36] The high school graduation rate for Perry Preschool children was 67%; for children in the control group, it was 49%.[37]

Studies on the short-term cognitive impact of Head Start are skewed. Over 30 studies have shown that Head Start enhances IQ, school readiness, and achievement test scores.[38] The intellectual advancements of Head Start children are generally nullified, however, within 3 years of their entry into the public-school system.[39] Because of the negative long-term cognitive outcomes recorded in the Head Start Synthesis Project, a compendium of Head Start studies, and other studies, the program has been criticized. It is true that the cognitive outcomes of Head Start children do not match the majority of the programs studied by the consortium. In contrast to Head Start, 9 of the 11 programs in the consortium were privately funded and professionally staffed. The expenditures per child in these private programs were significantly greater than the expenditures per child in Head Start.[40] Consequently, the private programs were able to fund a much higher quality early education experience. Moreover, the private programs offered an expanded quantitative program. The average duration of Head Start enrollment for a child is only 1 year. A child enrolled in Head Start for only a year cannot be expected to retain the benefits of the experience once enrolled in an elementary school in, say, the South Bronx, East Los Angeles, or, for that matter, just about any public elementary school catering primarily to low-income children.

There is a lack of socioemotional information on early education that extends beyond 10 years, but the results of the Perry Preschool and IDS programs are extremely favorable. A significant number of IDS children retained their linguistic skills, enhanced self-image, and sense of control.[41] Forty percent of the IDS children received college diplomas, compared with 27.5% of the children in the control group.[42] The percentage of IDS males employed full time was close to twice that of control-group males.[43]

The Perry Preschool children have been carefully monitored since their graduation from the program. At age 19, 38% of the Perry Preschool children were enrolled in college.[44] In contrast, only 21% of the control group attended college.[45] Half of the Perry Preschool children were employed, compared with 32% of the control group children.[46] The control group had welfare and arrest rates that were nearly double those of the Perry Preschool children.[47] Given these statistics, it was estimated that taxpayers saved at least $39,278 per child enrolled in the Perry Preschool program.[48]

Head Start and the Federal Response

The Human Services Reauthorization Act of 1990 was originally intended to allocate Head Start funds sufficient to enroll all eligible 3- and 4-year-olds and 30% of eligible 5-year-olds by 1994. Although Head Start has experienced a significant expansion, its funding has fallen far short of the amounts designated by the Human Services Reauthorization Act of 1990. Some legislators have proposed the School Readiness Act, which would provide Head Start services from birth to age 3. Other legislators and organizations have lobbied to give Head Start more of a transition role as the child enters elementary school.

The present administration seems to have focused its attention on enrolling 3- and 4-year-olds in Head Start. There are 1.8 million 3- and 4-year-olds living below the poverty threshold.[49] For a variety of reasons, it is generally conceded that 20% of the children eligible for Head Start will not be enrolled in the program. Consequently, administrators have extrapolated that full enrollment for 3- and 4-year-olds in Head Start is roughly 1.4 million. The federal government may allocate between $8 and $9 billion to Head Start for this population, which translates into approximately $6,000 per child.

If these numbers stand, the Head Start program may undergo an unprecedented increase in its expenditures per child—expeditures that are nearly on a par with other early education programs mentioned in this chapter. Such an increase will invariably enhance the program's quality, which has been a main concern of early education professionals. A higher quality Head Start experience for

3- and 4-year-olds will be at the expense, however, of thousands of children hovering just above the poverty threshold and thousands of other children outside the program's age parameters.

References

1. Washington V, Oyemade UJ. *Project Head Start: Past, Present and Future Trends in the Context of Family Values.* New York: Garland Publishing; 1987:8.

2. *Project Head Start Statistical Fact Sheet.* Washington, DC: US Dept of Health and Human Services, Administration for Children and Families; January 1993:3.

3. Ibid.

4. Ibid.

5. *Head Start: A Child Development Program.* Washington, DC: US Dept of Health and Human Services, Administration for Children and Families, Head Start Bureau; 1992:2–10.

6. Zigler E, Styfco S, Gilman E. *Head Start and Beyond: A National Plan for Extended Childhood Intervention.* New Haven: Yale University Press; 1993:26.

7. Ibid., 33.

8. Ibid., 41.

9. Ibid.

10. Whitebrook M, Howes C, Phillips D. *Who cares? Child care teachers and the quality of care in America.* Final Report on the National Child Care Staffing Study. Oakland, CA. Child Care Employee Project; 1989.

11. *Project Head Start Statistical Fact Sheet.* Washington, DC: US Dept of Health and Human Services, Administration for Children and Families; January 1993:2.

12. *The Future of Head Start.* Washington, DC: The Joint Economic Committee, Congress of the United States; 1990:13.

13. Jordan T et. al. Long-term effects of early enrichment: A 20-year perspective on persistence and change. *American Journal of Community Psychology.* 1985; 13:394.

14. Schweinhart L, Weikart D, *Early Childhood Education: Policy Issues for the 1990s.* Norwood, NJ: Ablex Publishing Corporation; 1992:71.

15. Jordan T et. al. Long-term effects of early enrichment: A 20-year perspective on persistence and change. *American Journal of Community Psychology.* 1985; 13:404.

16. *The Report of the Silver Ribbon Panel.* Alexandria, VA: National Head Start Association; 1991:33.

17. Ibid.

18. Collins RC, *Head Start Facilities Study.* Alexandria, VA: National Head Start Association; 1992:3.

19. Ibid.

20. Ibid., 15.

21. *The Report of the Silver Ribbon Panel.* Alexandria, VA: National Head Start Association; 1991:22.

22. McKey R et al. *The Impact of Head Start on Children, Families and Communities: Head Start Synthesis Project.* Washington, DC: US Dept of Health and Human Services; 1985:V-26.

23. *Project Head Start Statistical Fact Sheet.* Washington, DC: US Dept of Health and Human Services, Administration for Children and Families; January 1993:4.

24. Ibid.

25. McKey R et al. *The Impact of Head Start on Children, Families and Communities: Head Start Synthesis Project.* Washington, DC: US Dept of Health and Human Services; 1985:V-11.

26. Ibid.

27. Hale B, Seitz V, Zigler E. Health services and head start: A forgotten formula. *Journal of Applied Developmental Psychology.* 1990; 11:447–458.

28. Zigler E, Styfco E, Gilman E. *Head Start and Beyond: A National Plan for Extended Childhood Intervention.* New Haven: Yale University Press; 1993:15.

29. Haskins R. Beyond metaphor: The efficacy of early childhood education. *American Psychologist.* 1989; 4:275.

30. Ibid.

31. Ibid.

32. Jordan T et. al. Long-term effects of early enrichment: A 20-year perspective on persistence and change. *American Journal of Community Psychology.* 1985; 13:409.

33. Ibid.

34. Schweinhart L, Weikart D. *Early Childhood Education: Policy Issues for the 1990s.* Norwood, NJ: Ablex Publishing Corporation; 1992:68.

35. Ibid.

36. Ibid., 71.

37. Ibid.

38. McKey R et al. *The Impact of Head Start of Children, Families and Communities: Head Start Synthesis Project.* Washington, DC: US Dept of Health and Human Services; 1985:III-9.

39. Ibid., III-10–III-13.

40. Ibid., III-5.

41. Jordan T et. al. Long-term effects of early enrichment: A 20-year perspective on persistence and change. *American Journal of Community Psychology.* 1985; 13:411.

42. Ibid., 409.

43. Ibid.

44. Schweinhart L, Weikart D. *Early Childhood Education: Policy Issues for the 1990s.* Norwood, NJ: Ablex Publishing Corporation; 1992:71.

45. Ibid.

46. Ibid.

47. Ibid.

48. Ibid.

49. Unpublished Census data. March 1991 Current Population Survey, March Income Supplement, Table 23.

CHAPTER EIGHT

The Creation of an Integrated Children's Network

An aging US population is becoming increasingly dependent on an increasingly vulnerable and dysfunctional younger generation. If this trend continues, there is little doubt that the 21st century will be difficult. Unlike characters in the tragedies of ancient literature, however, we have control of our destiny. The escalation of poverty; the effects of hunger and homelessness; and the inadequacy of health care, child care, and early education services are barometers of our social will. Our new social will requires a renewed commitment to change and the realization that caring for our richest natural resource—children—is an investment in the truest sense of the word.

The following global principles and subsequent 20 recommendations address the requirements of our Integrated Children's Network (previously discussed in Chap. 1) from a unified perspective and from a component-specific perspective. The global principles will explain how the Integrated Children's Network can work as a unified apparatus. The specific recommendations will examine how current mechanisms can be improved to enhance and accommodate the six components of our Integrated Children's Network without the construction of elaborate new bureaucracies.

A Single, Unified Application Process

The fragmented and duplicative system of children's services must be replaced by an integrated system with a single point of entry. Specifically, a single application process and a unified application form would eliminate referrals to multiple sites (and multiple applications). Moreover, the development of an Integrated Children's Network with a single entry point will help to focus attention on the needs of our children and better integrate, coordinate, and fund the many children's programs that have been hard-hit over the past decade.

Accessibility and Choice

To counterbalance the single point of entry, an increased emphasis on choice is imperative. Eligibility for one service would automatically translate into eligibility for all six services. In the universally applicable Integrated Children's Network, a family entering the network through the WIC program or Head Start would be eligible for its full array of services. A financial worker or social worker acting under the auspices of the Aid to Families with Dependent Children (AFDC) program would help a family determine which of the components of the Integrated Children's Network match the family's particular needs. For example, health coverage and housing may not be major priorities for a family because of adequate coverage from the private sector, but it may require child care or early education services. As a family's needs change, it may need to use other components of the Integrated Children's Network. Although we are advocating an ideological paradigm shift to rectify the present problems of children, the actual mechanisms for the delivery of these services are already in place. An Integrated Children's Network would streamline programs rather than create another bureaucracy.

Standardized Financial Eligibility Criteria

At present, not only are children's services fragmented but their respective economic eligibility criteria are radically different. Each of the six components of the Integrated Children's Network would have standardized economic eligibility criteria. Services would be available to all those requiring assistance, including the corridor poor and the middle class. Contributions and the degree of subsidization would depend on family size and income, as dictated by federal poverty calculations. Families living below the federal poverty threshold would receive full benefits free of charge. Families with an income above 275% of the federal poverty threshold would have to pay in full for the services they utilize. The Integrated Children's Network acknowledges the needs of middle-class families and requires personal responsibility and accountability for all participating families. It displaces means-tested entitlements and categorical block grant programs by standarding eligibility benefits, which is welfare reform at its best. Figure 8.1 illustrates the sliding fee scale of the Integrated Children's Network.

Specific Recommendations for an Integrated Children's Network

Economic Security

1. There is a discrepancy between the states' present determination of the AFDC "standard of need" and payment levels provided to families receiving cash assistance. If an income threshold is determined to represent a standard of need or a minimal level of subsistence in a particular state, then that should be the amount of the payment allocated. Only 15 states grant AFDC recipients monthly

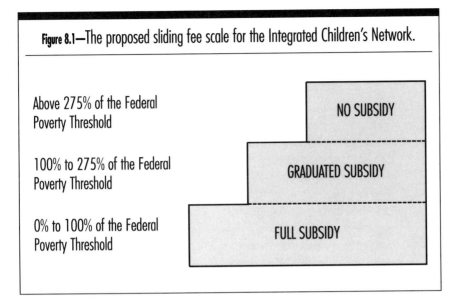

Figure 8.1—The proposed sliding fee scale for the Integrated Children's Network.

Above 275% of the Federal Poverty Threshold — NO SUBSIDY

100% to 275% of the Federal Poverty Threshold — GRADUATED SUBSIDY

0% to 100% of the Federal Poverty Threshold — FULL SUBSIDY

payments that match those states' minimum standard of need.[1]

2. Once the discrepancy between a state's standard of need and its actual payment is eliminated, a federal floor for cash assistance to families should be established. That floor would provide cash assistance at 50% of the federal poverty level. The AFDC payments of 38 states fall below 50% of the poverty threshold.[2] In Mississippi, for example, the cash allotment for a family of four is $144 a month.[3] Despite the federal floor, however, states would be able to provide cash assistance up to 100% of the federal poverty threshold.

3. The concept of a refundable child tax credit has been discussed by economists and public analysts over the past decade. The final report of the National Commission on Children advocated the replacement of the personal exemption with a $1000 refundable tax credit for all children under 18 years of age. In the Integrated Children's Network, the refundable child tax credit will be on a sliding scale, as follows:

- Families at or below the federal poverty threshold will receive $2000 a year per child.
- Families at 185% of the federal poverty threshold will receive $1000 a year per child.
- Families at 275% of the federal poverty threshold will receive $500 a year per child.
- Families over 275% of the federal poverty level will not receive a refundable tax credit.

Health Care

4. Medicaid has changed substantially since its enactment in 1965. It has evolved from a health insurance program for low-income Americans to the largest payer of nursing-home care. Medicaid

must be augmented by a universal health program for pregnant women and children up to 18 years of age. It would be made available to all children who lack coverage through the present employer-provided system. Employer coverage of dependent care would eventually be phased out and replaced by a single-payer program for maternity and child health care. There has been a protracted debate about the possibility of a US single-payer system. This approach would provide a model phased in with a distinct population, and the efficacy of such an approach could be evaluated rather easily.

5. Health care professionals—specifically physicians—should return to their historical mission, which is the promotion of health and the treatment of disease. Physicians and other health care providers should no longer be able to dismiss patients because of their economic status. Consequently, they should be required to treat both privately and publicly financed patients.

6. Enactment of the Child Health Insurance Reform Program (CHIRP) legislation is essential for the Integrated Children's Network. CHIRP, initially developed by the American Academy of Pediatrics, would alter insurance coverage within the private sector. Every insurance package would be required to provide preventive-care health services. A growing number of self-insuring employers are protected by the Employee Retirement Income Security Act (ERISA) of 1974 legislation, which exempts self-insured employers from certain state reg-

ulations and/or mandates of benefits. In opposition to ERISA, the Consolidated Omnibus Budget Reconciliation Act (COBRA) of 1985 has continuation and conversion provisions, which mandate that employers provide the opportunity for a person to maintain coverage through that person's former employer. CHIRP provisions should supersede ERISA in the same way COBRA supersedes ERISA. In other words, self-insuring employers would be required to cover preventive-care health services. Because we need a national commitment for full immunization of our preschool children, it is essential that this problem be addressed in both the public and private sectors.

Shelter

7. There are major gaps in the availability of affordable private housing and the availability of assisted housing. Since the early 1980s, the federal government has shifted its focus away from the construction, subsidization, and operation of public housing. In 1978, 32.1 billion federal dollars were appropriated for housing.[4] By 1988, however, only 9.8 billion federal dollars were appropriated for housing, which represents an 80% reduction in inflation-adjusted dollars.[5] In an effort to address the problem, local welfare agencies have been converted into de facto housing agencies. This strategy, however, generally produces inadequate, ad hoc housing solutions. An Integrated Children's Network would require housing and welfare agencies to work in concert with the private sector. Improving

these links would increase family stability and reduce homelessness by identifying the need for a housing-related intervention prior to or immediately after a setback that triggers homelessness.

8. Because shelter availability and costs are major barriers to self-sufficiency for low-income families, a reformed welfare system must focus on the transition to independence by providing secure, decent housing. The present housing policy serves but a fraction of the low-income families in need of housing or housing subsidization. An expansion of Section 8 certificates and the Department of Housing and Urban Development (HUD) Project Self-Sufficiency would help homeless families in search of permanent shelter.

9. In a September 1989 report, "Findings, Initiatives, and Recommendations," a joint advisory panel of the National Association of Housing and Redevelopment Officers and the American Public Welfare Association Advisory Panel issued a series of recommendations pertaining to the present increase in homeless families. Realizing the importance of integrated services, the panel proposed expanded support for family development programs in federally assisted housing, interim incentives for welfare families in transition, and coordinated programs (welfare and housing) at all levels of government.

Nutritional Support

10. The WIC and Food Stamp programs have been efficacious and cost-effective. We must ensure that all eligible low-income women, infants, and children receive assistance through the WIC program. The federal government cut $12.2 billion from the food stamp and child-nutrition programs from 1982 to 1985[6] by lowering federal subsidies, altering income-eligibility criteria, and increasing the amount that families had to pay for a meal. WIC is a discretionary program: it is limited by a federal ceiling. Consequently, WIC serves only 55% of those who are eligible.[7] According to a Community Childhood Hunger Identification Project (CCHIP) survey, 31% of those who were eligible for the WIC program and not receiving WIC benefits were hungry or at risk of hunger.[8] Given WIC's importance, all families earning less than 275% of the federal poverty threshold should be eligible for the program.

11. Participation in the National School Lunch Program has declined. In 1980, for example, 27 million children were participating; by 1990, however, that number had dwindled to 24.5 million.[9] The School Breakfast Program has suffered a similar fate. Only 53% of the schools offering a lunch program offer a breakfast program.[10] Federal, state, and local policies should ensure that the National School Breakfast Program is as accessible to low-income children as the National School Lunch Program. The availability of meals for low-income children under the age of 5 who are not enrolled in school should be expanded

through the Child and Adult Care Food Program and the Summer Food Service Program for Children.

Child Care

12. After an arduous legislative battle in 1990, the 101st Congress enacted the Child Care and Development Block Grant and the At-Risk Child Care Programs. The Child Care and Development Block Grant allocates $2.5 billion for low-income child care over three years. Since 34 million children under 13 years of age are without a regular source of childcare, this 1990 legislation is only a beginning.[11] Because 75% of the funds generated by the Child Care and Development Block Grant and the At-Risk Child Care Programs are funneled to low-income families, the legislation will have only a minor impact on US child care problems.[12] Our government's lack of child care intervention throughout the 1980s and early 1990s has contributed to the inability of many families to pay for needed child care. Child care programs such as Social Services Block Grant under Title XX, the Child Care Development Block Grant, and the At-Risk Child Care Programs should be consolidated. Increased money allocations from the federal government will also be necessary.

13. If the United States is to have a rational child care policy, the federal government must determine definitive minimum standards for child care facilities receiving federal subsidies or tax considerations. Efforts to enact a set of federal child care quality and safety stan-

dards ended in 1981 when the Social Service Block Grant replaced Title XX of the Social Security Act. Consequently, these programs reverted to state licensing and registration requirements. For the most part, state standards have followed successive federal leads since the 1960s, and many states require far lower standards than years of research and hearings show are needed. A few states exempt some or all church-operated programs from licensing or registration requirements. Our society inspects and monitors food, drugs, water, and the environment, but we place infants, toddlers, and preschoolers in the care of people who are not obligated to conform to standards defined by professionals and experts in the child care field.

14. A discussion of future child care services would be incomplete without mention of the inadequate salaries now paid to caregivers. The upgrading of salaries and work conditions for center and family day-care personnel is essential if turnover rates of 50% are to be reduced. Because child care is typically a minimum-wage job, well trained professionals are discouraged from entering or remaining in the field. The provision of federal scholarships and training funds would help to ensure that the child care field has a vibrant, competent work force.

15. Investment in research, evaluation, and demonstration projects that employ new and innovative methodologies in child care programming is imperative. Although officials have allocated

funds to demonstration projects, they have approved only those proposals that reflect their ideological positions. Consequently, their efforts provide few authentic opportunities to test alternative and competing theories and models. Because state planners have been hampered by a scarcity of data about child care methodologies, a child care database would be an innovative way to enhance research and evaluation.

Head Start

16. An expansion of the Head Start Training and Technical Assistance network is important in maintaining quality. The Training and Technical Assistance network provides on-site training designed to meet the specific needs of individual programs. These specific needs generally include training in priority areas such as services to handicapped children, technical assistance, newsletters, and other issues pertaining to current trends.

17. Head Start programs must be staffed properly to meet their multidimensional purpose. In recent years, Head Start staff have expressed concern over the growing number of multiproblem families enrolling in the program. Such families place increased demands on staff time for activities such as one-on-one counseling, assistance to parents, and extra home visits. If Head Start is to continue to provide comprehensive services to low-income children, Head Start staff must be increased.

18. To meet the additional needs of low-income children and families, Head Start transition programs should collaborate with other early childhood programs, human services providers, and the business community. Because of the increasing concern that the cognitive progress made by Head Start children may be lost when comprehensive services are discontinued in the school, there must be full implementation of Head Start transition projects.

19. Over the past 15 years, the percentage of the Head Start budget devoted to research, demonstration, and evaluation has diminished radically. In 1974, 2.5% of the overall Head Start budget was used for research and experimentation; by 1989, this percentage had diminished to 0.11%. Current Head Start policy is predicated on research conducted on programs designed years ago. Because the problems faced by children and families change, updated research is needed to inform decision makers on policy issues.

20. Over the past decade, Head Start programs have suffered a shortage of affordable and appropriate facilities. Many of Head Start's landlords are no longer willing to donate space and, in many cases, landlords are asking for commercial rates. In addition, because of an expanding preschool population, public schools have taken back space that they had formerly donated or rented to Head Start programs. The General Accounting Office estimates that 29% of Head Start's facilities are located in public school buildings. It is essential that

Head Start have the resources to purchase adequate facilities.

The above recommendations are needed to improve the potential of America's children to grow and develop. This will entail the investment of significant resources and those investments should be based on the merit of each recommendation. The establishment of an integrated children's network will help to ensure a child's future autonomy. However, other broad societal factors such as family structure, community violence, and education are of critical importance.

References

1. *Green Book: Overview of Entitlement Programs,* Washington, DC: US House of Representatives, Committee on Ways and Means. GPO publication 102–44; 1992:641–644.

2. Ibid.

3. Ibid.

4. Blau J. *The Visible Poor.* New York: Oxford University Press; 1992:71-72.

5. Ibid.

6. *Hunger in the United States.* Washington, DC: Campaign to End Childhood Hunger; 1992:2.

7. Ibid., 7.

8. *A Survey of Childhood Hunger in the United States (Executive Summary).* Washington, DC: Community Childhood Hunger Identification Project; 1991.

9. *Annual Historical Review of FNS Programs.* Washington, DC: US Dept of Agriculture; 1991:369.

10. *School Breakfast Score Card.* Washington, DC: Food Research and Action Center; 1992:12.

11. *The Demand and Supply of Child Care in 1990.* Washington, DC: National Association for the Education of Young Children; 1992:16.

12. Zigler E, Gillman E. Day care in America: What is needed? *Pediatrics.* January 1993; 1:176.

CHAPTER NINE

A Child's Right to Autonomy

" Autonomy then is the basis of the dignity of human and of every rational nature...."

—IMMANUEL KANT

A truly autonomous person acts in accordance with a freely chosen and informed plan, remaining free from both controlling interference by others and personal limitations that would prevent meaningful choices. In contrast, a person of limited autonomy is controlled by others or is unable to deliberate or act on his or her inclinations. Because autonomy is a requisite for freedom and liberty, US citizens have viewed autonomy as a preeminent value and an essential social good to which all persons are entitled.

The proposed Integrated Children's Network can give an underserved child the potential for developing into an autonomous person. Chapters 3 through 8 have demonstrated the importance of each component in the six-part paradigm. After we examine the negative medical, cognitive, and socioemotional impacts of inadequate health care, shelter, nutrition, child care, and early education, it is obvious that underserved children are not being granted the tools to become autonomous adults. Consequently, if the United States is to ensure each child the potential to become an autonomous adult, it must meet each child's basic needs.

There are many factors in the US psyche that have prevented underserved children from becoming competent adults and, thus, autonomous individuals. A political ideology grounded in distinguishing the "deserving" from the "undeserving" poor is one such factor. The ideas about the "deserving" and "undeserving" poor are based in the Elizabethan poor laws of the colonial era. Those laws identified two poor populations. The deserving poor included the impoverished elders, underfed children, and the unemployable blind and disabled who were neither blamed for their condition nor envied for being the recipients of relief. The undeserving poor were thought to be parasitic paupers who were entirely responsible for their abject condition.

Aid to Dependent Children (ADC), or Title IV of the Social Security Act of 1935, which was the prototype of the Aid to Families with Dependent Children (AFDC) program, was firmly entrenched in the ideological position that distinguished the deserving from the undeserving poor. Consequently, the program supplemented the needs of only those children who were considered to be among the deserving poor. After 1950, however, the ADC program was transformed into AFDC, or what is commonly called "welfare." The inequitable treatment of AFDC adults—and consequently their children—is linked to a negative view of the poor: that the adults of the AFDC population are largely responsible for their situation and are therefore undeserving.

In contrast to the AFDC population, the elderly and disabled have powerful lobbying groups to ensure that the federal government finances their proliferating needs. Medicaid, for example, funds nearly 43% of all nursing-home expenditures in this country.[1] Consequently, the powerful nursing-home lobbies vigorously resist policy changes that would result in a decline in revenues for the elderly and disabled. The private sector would lose a great deal of money if the government withdrew its support from this population. Children and poor families are not nearly as lucrative to health care providers and have far less political clout than the aged and the disabled. In addition, political advocates for children and poor families have not attained the political status to force policymakers to address their concerns. Thus, in a political scenario, it is reasonable to assume that the aged and the disabled receive preferential treatment over the AFDC population.

The social position perpetuated by the myth of the deserving and undeserving poor and the impact of lobbies played an integral role in the Social Security Amendments of 1972. This legislation gave the aged, the blind, and the disabled a federal standard for their payments. In contrast, AFDC payments were to be dictated solely by individual states. Payments for the supplemental security income (SSI) population are indexed to keep pace with inflation, and they are approximately 90% of the federal poverty level. The average AFDC payment is approximately 50% of the poverty level.[2]

Additional inequities between the adults of the AFDC and SSI populations result from sexism and racism. In Chapter 3, we showed that minority children living in female-headed households were disproportionately represented among underserved children. In 1991, the poverty rates for Blacks, Hispanics, and Whites were 32.7%, 28.7%, and 11.3%, respectively.[3] Women constitute two-thirds of all poor adults in the United States.[4] Nearly 75% of full-time working women earn less than $20,000 a year, which is not quite half the amount men earn, and women are twice as likely not to draw a pension.[5] The average female college graduate earns less than a male who has only a high school diploma.

Given the racist and sexist dynamics of our society, it is not surprising that almost 50% of Black and Hispanic children in female-headed households are living in poverty.[6]

According to Immanuel Kant, a person must be treated as an end and not a means if he or she is to be autonomous.[7] A person who is treated as an end or as intrinsically valuable, will not be viewed merely as an instrument to achieve the purposes of another person, group, or institution. Only a person who is treated as an end will be able to exercise fully the capacity for making choices.

According to Kant, an autonomous existence is not only a right, it is a duty that humans owe their fellow humans.[8] If we strip a person of his or her autonomy, not only are we demeaning that person, but we are also demeaning ourselves, because it is our responsibility to treat people as an end in themselves and, consequently, as autonomous individuals. The explosion of service-sector jobs throughout the 1980s is a fitting example of people being treated merely as a means for their employers' profitmaking. In many instances, they are paid minimum wage and seldom offered pensions, profit sharing, health-insurance coverage, or disability coverage.

Although the majority of US workers are treated as a means to an end, they have the power when acting in solidarity to demand concessions from their employers because of their importance in the production and distribution of commodities. Moreover, they have the potential to demand concessions through the ballot box. Because children do not take part in the production and distribution of commodities or the electoral process, they cannot demand concessions from employers or the government. Children do not even represent a means to an end in a sociopolitical system obsessed with short-term outcomes. In other words, children are neglected because too many people in our society view them as having little to offer in the short term.

Because children cannot exercise their rights to self-determination, freedom of choice, informed course of action, and effective deliberation, they are a dependent and vulnerable population. Therefore, it is the duty of society to provide our children with adequate health care, shelter, nutrition, child care, and early education. If children are denied what should be their entitlements, their potential to become autonomous adults will be either jeopardized or negated. If the inequities documented in this book continue without federal intervention, a large segment of our children will be at risk, and we will bear the responsibility for their fate.

References

1. Oberg C, Polich C. Medicaid—Entering the third decade. *Health Affairs.* 1988; 7:89.

2. Bach M, Oberg C, Bryant N. Ethics and medicaid: A new look at an old problem. *Journal of Health Care for the Poor and Underserved;* 1992:2:433.

3. *Poverty in the United States: 1991.* Washington, DC: US Bureau of the Census; 1992: vii-ix. Current Populations Reports, Series P-60, No. 181.

4. Faludi S. *Backlash: The Undeclared War Against Women.* New York: Anchor Books; 1991:xiii.

5. Ibid.

6. *Poverty in the United States: 1991.* Washington, DC: US Bureau of the Census; 1992: Table 1. Current Populations Reports, Series P-60, No. 181.

7. Kant I. *Fundamental Principles of the Metaphysic of Morals.* Chicago: University of Chicago Press; 1950; 9-10.

8. Ibid.